Getting Home Alive

Getting Home Alive

by Aurora Levins Morales and Rosario Morales

Firebrand
Books
Ithaca, New York

Selections from this book have appeared previously in the following books and periodicals: *Areto; Coming Up!; Cuentos, Stories by Latinas,* edited by Alma Gómez, Cherríe Moraga, and Mariana Romo-Carmona (Kitchen Table: Women of Color Press); *Puerto Rico Libre!; Reflections: The Anthropological Muse,* edited by Ian Pettis; *Sojourner; This Bridge Called My Back, Writings by Radical Women of Color,* edited by Cherríe Moraga and Gloria Anzaldúa (Kitchen Table: Women of Color Press); and *WREE-View.*

The excerpt from "Borderlands" by Gloria Anzaldúa is from a forthcoming book by the same name to be published by Spinsters-Aunt Lute.

Book and cover design by Mary A. Scott
Cover art by Rosario Morales
Typesetting by Bets Ltd.

Printed on acid-free paper in the United States by McNaughton & Gunn

This publication is made possible, in part, with support from the Literature Panel, New York State Council on the Arts.

Library of Congress Cataloging-in-Publication Data

Morales, Aurora Levins, 1954-
  Getting home alive.

  1. American literature—Puerto Rican authors.
2. American literature—Jewish authors.   3. American
literature—Women authors.   4. American literature—
20th century.   5. Puerto Rican women—Literary
collections.   6. Feminism—Literary collections.
I. Morales, Rosario, 1930-   II. Title.
PS508.P84M67   1986   818'.5408   86-22769
ISBN 0-932379-20-6 (alk. paper)
ISBN 0-932379-19-2 (pbk. : alk. paper)

Introduction/Acknowledgments

This book began in long budget-breaking telephone calls stretched across the width of this country, in "listen to what I've just written"; in "did you hear about this book, this song, this poem, this event?" It began because Rosario wrote rhymes at eleven and not again until she was in her forties and Aurora wrote poetic thoughts when she was seven and was a working writer and teacher when her mother started up again, each influencing the other willy-nilly, through the good times and the bad, the fights and the making up, the long sullen silences and the happy chatter cluttering the phone line strung between us like a 3000-mile umbilical cord from navel to navel, mine to hers, hers to mine, each of us mother and daughter by turns, feeding each other the substance of our dreams.

I give thanks to:

Nancy Bereano who instigated this book and without whom, for sure, it would still be a dream burning the telephone wires between Oakland and Cambridge;

Avis Cohen and the Ithaca Poets for bringing Nancy and our poetry together;

My mother for her stories, her gossip, her language, her pride in me;

My father for his immense vocabulary in English, his pride in Spanish, and the copy of *Hamlet*;

My husband and best friend, Dick Levins, the only person to hear first drafts of everything I write, for his love, support and unfailing enthusiasm;

My typists Neenyah Ostrom, Rachael Nasca, and MacIntosh;
My teachers, especially Joan Larkin;
My writing groups, the first one with Linda Stein, Aileen Brill, Katie Sawyer, Kim, and E. J. Graff; the second, the third world one, with Julia Perez, Kate Rushin, Beverly Smith, and Margaret Braxton, and this latest one, particularly the three women, Helen Horrigan, Chantal Lévi Alvarès-Fujiwara, and Laura Derr of its latest incarnation;
Cherríe Moraga for the appreciation and critique of my early work that inspired me to continue;
Suzanne Motheral, Chantal Lévi Alvarès-Fujiwara, Grey Cahill, and Samuel Aponte for being good loving friends who praise my writing, Mary Lowry for loving "Origins of Racism," Martin Espada, Camilo Perez, Marjory Agosín for their encouragement and for getting me my latina/o audiences; Norma Exler and Laura Jacubowitz, wherever you are;
To my wonderful family Gloria, Jandro — my sometimes agent, Cardo, Paula, Olivia, Jim;
And last but hardly least, to Aurora, my first-born child, mentor, teacher and coauthor.

Rosario (Sari) Morales
Cambridge, MA
May 1986

Introduction/Acknowledgments

My mother was the one who taught me to read. I was five, and the magical process by which shapes on the page became filled with meaning so I could unlock their stories was one of the all-time thrills of my life. She taught me to read, and she read me all her favorite children's books and soon the adult books, the Gilbert and Sullivan, the Dickens. The first rule I remember learning was never to harm or deface a book. The second was never to cross a picket line.

My mother taught me to read. I remember her prowling the house at night when she was insomniac. The sound of tea water climbing to a boil and pages turning. Then she would pass my door with a steaming mug of tea and a book open in her other hand. She taught me to love the women: Jane Austen, Dorothy Sayers, Josephine Tey, Virginia Woolf, and later we would trade the titles of new books on the phone: Doris Lessing, Agnes Smedley, Charlotte Bronte's *Shirley,* June Jordan, Toni Morrison, Alice Walker. "I found a great new book, a new author, have you read...?"

At some point, interwoven with our book reviews, we began to read each other our writing as well. "I have a new piece...whaddya think?" Often we heard the pieces long before anyone else did, in their earliest, most fragile incarnations, and over and over again we cried to hear the stories told, the power reclaimed, the emerging voices strengthening.

We aren't exempt from the hard times. Like other mothers and daughters we have our yelling matches, the anger and silences between us. But we have always had this, too: that we are teachers to each other, that we love the power of our own and each other's lives, that we are able to see beyond the mother-daughter knot to where the bond is. There, we walk out of the house in Chicago not speaking to each other and drive to the feminist meeting in silence, where we fight like hell for each other in the face of ageism and adultism because we are a little too young and old respectively. There, we join forces to think about the world, about women's lives, and about how being who we are has shaped us. There, we send each other postcards of women writing, write about each other's lives, read each other's work to audiences and friends.

This book is the blossoming of that cross-fertilization. My mother taught me how to read. Together, we have taught ourselves to be writers.

Thanks to Nancy Bereano, who took this book off the phone lines and into print, years sooner than it would have happened without her.

Many women and men nurtured me in various ways through the writing of this book: they expected the best from me, called me up to see how it was going, listened to my drafts, commiserated with me, soothed my anxieties, told me my work mattered, and made me cups of tea: Marcy Alancraig, Gus Bagakis, Gail Boehm, Kim Chernin, Laura Davis, Nola Hadley, Katherine Hazard, Alison Ehara Brown, Marty Johnson, Irena Klepfisz, Lisa Kokin, Alejandro Levins Morales, Ricardo Levins Morales, Richard Levins, Bill Mack, Ruth Mahaney, Christian McEwen, Judit Moschkovich, Jim Otis, Annie Popkin, Paula Ross, Ricky Sherover-Marcuse, Tasha Silver, Deborah Stone, Donna Warnock.

Also thanks to my first grade teacher Eleanor West, of Rochester, NY, who believed every child could write poetry, and to my ninth grade teacher, Darlene Friedman, of Chicago, who gave me and Kathy Hazard the editorship of a tiny, dittoed literary magazine and took us seriously.

Shortly after we agreed to do this book I was in a car accident and injured my brain. For a year I was unable to think abstractly, plan tasks, remember what I was doing, remember the names of objects, speak clearly, or sometimes even write my name. My partner, Jim Otis, took care of me, supported me, believed absolutely that I would return to speech and writing, and worked for my healing in dozens of ways. Jan Corwin, my speech therapist, guided me back, step by step, with spunky affection. My heartfelt thanks to both of them, and to the staff of the Mt. Diablo Rehabilitation Center.

Aurora (Lori) Levins Morales
Oakland, CA
May 1986

Table of Contents

Editor's Note

This book is coauthored by Aurora Levins Morales (Lori) and Rosario Morales (Sari). Each selection is appropriately credited in the Table of Contents, as indicated below.

In order to distinguish their work visually, the book is typeset in two typefaces: Signature, the first paragraph of this note, for Aurora's writing, and Clearface, the typeface of this paragraph, for Rosario's.

To live in the Borderlands means
    the mill with the razor sharp teeth
    wants to shred off your olive-red skin
    crush out the kernel, your heart
    pound you pinch you roll you out
    smelling like white bread but dead

To live in the Borderlands means
    you are at home, a stranger wherever you are
    the border disputes have been settled
    the volley of shots have shattered the truce
    you are wounded, lost in action
    fighting back, a survivor.

To survive the Borderlands means
    you must live *sin fronteras*
    be a crossroads

                                Gloria Anzaldúa

Living
In
The
Borderlands

Wolf

I am in a clay house with whitewashed walls. It's dark. Outside, lightning is flashing and rain is falling. Lightning blazing behind it, a wolf appears in the doorway. I greet it with an upwelling of the deepest joy in my heart. This is my true self. As it moves toward me it changes shapes, becomes buffalo, becomes anteater, always flickering back to its true shape of a wolf. It is changing shape to protect itself from extinction, but I realize all the animals it changes into are also endangered. Then I am sitting in the middle of a dark plain, around a campfire. Those near me are younger, more unaware. I try to tell them, "My totem is the wolf," but they don't know what a wolf is. They have never seen one. I say, "It's like those dogs with the curly tails," meaning huskies, and they nod, bored, not really paying attention. They think I mean a dog. I say, "But you can't imagine the utter wildness and beauty of a wolf." They don't understand me and I know it is urgently, desperately important. For their survival and mine and the world's, I must make them see the wolf's nature. I must tell them this story.

Getting Out Alive

1.

The South Bronx appears on the TV screen:
I'm looking down Beck Street toward my block.
I stare in shock.

Oh, I'd known things were rough there
After I left,
And that after my parents left it was called Korea
That it was a war zone of sorts.
I'd known
and I hadn't known.

God!
On both sides of the street houses are leveled
Rubble lies on the ground.
Where the grocery store stood—only rubble on an empty lot.
Buildings empty
Their bare plumbing showing through the wounds in the walls
Tile floors covered with plaster and porcelain.
Houses lying there helpless
while children enter and poke and hurt
Use her as a latrine.

I look quickly toward Tiffany
Searching for my old home.
The picture flicks
away.

2.

I moved away from El Barrio
I moved away from the Bronx
I left when the signs showed increasing danger.

Stores with large boards across their gashed windows
Streets full of debris, paper blowing into doorways
I knew the signs,
The smell of death permeating the brick like urine
The occasional casualty spilling brick and glass onto the pavement.
Did I get out in time?

3. Refugee

Get out before the bombs hit your house!
Get out before the soldiers come to rape and kill!

The road full of refugees on foot, their lives pushed wearily in front
of them in baby carriages, in carts which they pull like horses. Only
here and there a car, unable to move any faster than the slowest
walkers. A plane appears. Darts toward us. Scatter! Hide! Bullets rain
down. Pull your head closer to the ground. A bomb leaves a hole
where people and whole households in bags and carts were moving
to safety. Get up! Go faster! Leave something else behind! Now only
getting out alive matters.

4.

Listen, little girl
The good guys don't strafe.
They don't bomb civilians.
They don't kill women and children.
American democracy defends you against those things
Defends you against the evil men who do things like that.

I believed that. I believed that while I scanned the landscape before
I walked it to make sure there were no marauders. While I scanned
the landscape for signs of increasing danger.
Look before you walk.

5.

What have they done to El Barrio? Where are the low houses teeming with people, the streets full of women walking arm in arm, of families standing in front of the candy store, girls playing double dutch or bouncing a ball beneath their swinging legs, boys and girls running in and out of the fire hydrant's barreling waters.
Do you see it? Smell it?
The men in their undershirts sitting on the stoops drinking beer,
The women leaning on their elbows out of the open windows watching the scene go by,
The smell of ripe plátano frying,
The fight overheard, through the first story window,
Listen!
The streets full of life and sound, singing shouting greeting.
"¿Que tal? ¿Y cómo estas, chica?"
"¡Tita! ¡Ven acá enseguida! ¡Te estoy llamando hace media hora!"
"¡Fea, fea, tu eres fea!"
"No, m'hija. Hace tiempo que no la veo. A que se fué pa Puerto Rico. Si no tenia pa que quedarse."
"¡Malcriá, deja que te coja! ¡Esa niña me la voy a comer!"
The high rapid fire of Puerto Rican speech with the softness of dropped syllables and consonants, round and soft and familiar. The laughing: high loud laughter out of wide open mouths.

6. Leave Something Else Behind

I cried when I heard my voice on tape for the first time. My voice showed no signs of El Barrio, of the South Bronx. I had erased them, helped my teachers erase the signs that I had been a little girl from the tenements who couldn't speak a word of English when she went to kindergarten, not even to say, "I need to pipi, I'll wet my pants," to say, "I'm scared, I want to go home."

Gone.

Only a detective cunning and suspicious could discover what is left
of my former life in my speech.

7.

I moved to Chicago
A city of casual death reported daily on the radio:
Three young Black men shot in the night, one dying.
The first people we meet:
One has just come out of the hospital
His face smashed in with a brick.
A man wanted the money in his wallet.
My son held up at gunpoint in a doorway—
He had only change to give.

And rape.
Barbara raped, Linda raped, Marcia raped, Judy almost raped.
Someone was shot on 55th Street
Someone was stabbed a few blocks from my home.

The streets full of prowling police cars
Looking for prey.

Don't go out alone at night
        Carry a whistle
Lock the door
        Lock the windows
Lock yourself
Lock yourself up
Lock yourself up—shut.

8.

The TV program about the South Bronx showed a young Puerto Rican man, an adolescent. He said his father had been stabbed seventeen times right in front of his eyes, that someone had held him back, that no one had helped his father, that the cops had looked the other way.

9.

I wear a yellow star behind my heart
    above my liver
I still hear Guernica burning
Yesterday I walked the dusty miles to a hungry reservation.
Today I staggered from Shatila bleeding.

I have changed my name
    my religion
    my family
    my language
I have run away from the persecution that is always all around me.
It is always all around me.
I am never safe,
never safe.

10. The Dream

All my relatives were herded into a department store, all except me. I rode in the jeep with the stormtrooper with the blond hair and I pretended to be white and blond and Aryan and "O.K." The stormtrooper washed the chain-link fence around the store with a hose that spouted clean clear water and water streamed out of my eyes but nothing could wash me clean. My aunt Mercedes was in the department store and Mercedes stayed in the Bronx and I walked away on a sunny day with the hose playing and the water sparkling as it fell.

Immigrants

For years after we left Puerto Rico for the last time, I would wake from a dream of something unbearably precious melting away from my memory as I struggled desperately to hold on, or at least to remember that I had forgotten. I am an immigrant, and I forget to feel what it means to have left. What it means to have arrived.

There was hail the day we got to Chicago and we joked that the city was hailing our arrival. The brown brick buildings simmered in the smelly summer, clenched tight all winter against the cold and the sooty sky. It was a place without silence or darkness, huddled against a lake full of dying fish whose corpses floated against the slime-covered rocks of the south shore.

Chicago is the place where the slack ended. Suddenly there was no give. In Indiera there was the farm: the flamboyan tree, the pine woods, the rainforest hillsides covered with alegría, the wild joyweed that in English is called impatiens. On the farm there were hideouts, groves of bamboo with the tiny brown hairs that stuck in your skin if you weren't careful. Beds of sweet-smelling fern, drowsymaking under the sun's heat, where the new leaves uncurled from fiddleheads and tendrils climbed and tangled in a spongy mass six feet deep. There were still hillsides, out of range of the house, where I could watch lizards hunt and reinitas court, and stalk the wild cuckoos, trying to get up close. There were mysteries and consolations. There was space.

Chicago was a wasteland. Nowhere to walk that was safe. Killers and rapists everywhere. Police sirens. Ugly, angry looks. Bristling hostility. Worst of all, nowhere to walk. Nowhere to go if it was early morning and I had to get out. Nowhere to go in the late afternoon or in the gathering dusk that meant fireflies and moths at home. Nowhere to watch animal life waking into a new day. The animal life was rats and dogs, and they were always awake because it never got dark here; always that sickly purple and orange glow they call sky in this place. No forest to run wild in. Only the lot across 55th Street with huge piles of barren earth, outlines of old cellars, and a few besieged trees in a scraggly row. I named one of them Ceres, after the goddess of earth and plenty who appeared in my high school production of *The Tempest:* bounteous Ceres, queen of the wasteland. There were no hills to race down, tumbling into heaps of fern, to slide down, on a slippery banana leaf; no place to get muddy. Chicago had grime, but no mud. Slush, but no slippery places of the heart, no genuine moistness. Only damp alleyways, dank brick, and two little humps in the middle of 55th Street over which grass had been made to grow. But no real sliding. No slack.

There are generations of this desolation behind me, desolation, excitement, grief, and longing all mixed in with the dirty air, the noise, seasickness, and the strangeness of wearing a winter coat.

My grandmother Lola was nineteen the day she married my grandfather and sailed away to Nueva York in 1929. She had loved someone else, but his family disapproved and he obeyed their orders to leave for the States. So her family married her to a son of a neighboring family because the family store was doing poorly and they could no longer support so many children. Two months after her first love left, she found herself married and on the boat. She says: "I was a good Catholic girl. I thought it was my duty to marry him, that it was for the good of my family." I have pictures of her, her vibrant beauty wrapped up but not smothered in the winter coats and scarves, in my grandfather's violent possessiveness and jealousy. She is standing in Central Park with her daughters, or with her arms around a friend or cousin. Loving the excitement. Loving the neighbors and the hubbub. In spite of racist landlords. In spite of the girdle factory. In spite of Manolin's temper and the poverty and hunger. Now, retired to Manolin's dream of a little house in Puerto Rico with a yard and many plants to tend, she longs for New York or some other U.S. city where a woman can go out and about on her own, live among many voices speaking different languages, out of the stifling air of that house, that community, that family.

My mother, the child in that Central Park photo, grew up an immigrant child among immigrants. She went to school speaking not a word of English, a small Puerto Rican girl scared out of her wits, and learned fast: learned accentless English in record time, the sweet cadence of her mother's open-voweled words ironed out of her vocabulary, the edges flattened down, made crisp, the curls and flourishes removed. First generation.

The strangeness. The way time worked differently. The way being on time mattered. Four second bells. Four minutes of passing time between classes. A note from home if you were ten minutes late, which you took to the office and traded for a late pass. In Indiera the classroom emptied during coffee season, and they didn't bother to send the inspector up unless we were out for longer than four or five weeks. No one had a clock with a second hand. We had half days of school because there were only four rooms for six grades. Our room was next to the bakery, and the smell of the warm pan de agua filled our lungs and stomachs and mouths. Things happened when they were ready, or "cuando Dios quiere." The público to town, don Paco's bread, the coffee ripening, the rain coming, growing up.

The stiffness. The way clothing mattered with an entirely different kind of intensity. In Indiera, I wore the same wine-colored jumper to school each day with the same white blouse, and only details of the buttons or the quality of the cloth or the presence or absence of earrings, only the shoes gave information about the homes we left at dawn each day, and I was grateful to be able to hide my relative wealth. In Chicago, there were rituals I had never heard of. Knee socks and plaid skirts and sweaters matching each other according to a secret code I didn't understand. Going steady and wearing name tags. First date, second date, third date, score. The right songs to be listening to. The right dances. The coolness.

In the middle of coolness, of stiffness, of strangeness, my joyful rushing up to say, "I come from Puerto Rico, a nest of beauty on the top of a mountain range." Singing "beauty, beauty, beauty." Trying to get them to see in their minds' eyes the perfect edge of a banana leaf against a tropical blue sky, just wanting to speak of what I longed for. Seeing embarrassed faces turning away, getting the jeering voices, singing "Puerto Riiiico, my heart's devotion . . . let it sink into the ocean!" Learning fast not to talk about it, learning excruciatingly slowly how to dress, how to act, what to say, where to hide. The exuberance, the country-born freshness going quietly stale. Made flat. Made palatable. Made unthreatening. Not different, really. Merely "exotic."

I can remember the feelings, but I forget to give them names. In high school we read novels about immigrant families. In college we discussed the problems of other first generations, talked about displacement, talked about families confused and divided, pride and shame. I never once remembered that I was an immigrant, or that both my parents are the first U.S.-born generations of their families.

My father is the First American Boy. His mother, Ruth, was born in Russia. Took the boat with her mother, aunt, and uncle when she was two. My grandfather Reuben was the second son of Lev Levinsky, the first one born in the new country, but born into the ghetto. Lev and the first son, Samuel, were orthodox, old-country Jews, but Reuben and his younger brother Ben went for the new. They worked three or four jobs at once. They ran a deli in shifts and went to law school in their free hours. So Rube grew up and out of the immigrant poverty, still weak and bent from childhood hungers, still small and vulnerable. The sicker he got, the harder he worked to safeguard his wife and sons, adding on yet another job, yet another project until he worked himself to death at the age of forty-six.

My father was the First American Boy: the young genius, the honors student, the PhD scientist. Each milestone recorded in home movies. His letters and report cards hoarded through the decades, still exhibited to strangers. The one who knew what was what. The expert. The one who carried the family spark, the one to boast about. The one with the weight of the family's hope on his shoulders. First generation.

And what am I?

The immigrant child of returned immigrants who repeated the journey in the second generation. Born on the island with first-hand love and the stories of my parents' Old Country—New York; and behind those, the secondhand stories of my mother's father, of the hill town of his long-ago childhood, told through my mother's barrio childhood. Layer upon layer of travel and leaving behind, an overlay of landscapes, so that I dream of all the beloved and hated places, and endlessly of trains and paths and roads and ships docking and leaving port and a multitude of borders and officials waiting for my little piece of paper.

I have the passport with which my great-grandmother Leah, traveling as Elisavieta, and her sister Betty (Rivieka) and her brother Samuel and her mother Henke and my grandmother Riva, a round two-year-old to be known all her life as Ruth, and a neighbor who traveled with them as a relative, all came together into New York. I touch the seal of Russia, the brown ink in which their gentile names were recorded, the furriness of the old paper, the place where the date is stamped: June 1906. My great-grandfather Abe had come alone, fleeing the draft, by way of England and Canada, two years earlier.

I don't know what it looked like, the Old Country they left, the little farm in the Ukraine. I will never know. The town of Yaza was utterly destroyed in two gory days in 1942, eight thousand shot and buried in long trenches. My aunt Betty was unable to speak by the time I wanted to ask her: What was it like, a girl of fifteen, to come from that countryside to New York, to suddenly be working ten hours a day in a factory? I have the tiniest fragments, only the dust clinging to their shoes. The dreamy look on my great-grandmother's face one morning when I was ten, watching me play jacks. "There was a game we used to play on the farm, just like that, but with round little stones from the river, tossed from the fronts to the backs of our hands: how many times before they fall?" Pop's, my great-grandfather's painting of the farm he grew up on, and a dozen pages he left in phonetic yiddishy English about the place he grew up in, the horses, the pumpkins, the potatoes, the family decision for him to marry, to flee to New York, where you had to use *tsikolodzi* (psychology) to stay on top.

My grandmother Ruth unexpectedly answering my questions about her earliest memories with a real story, one whole, shining piece of her life: *"Dancing. We were on the boat from Russia. The sun was shining. The place we slept was smelly, stuffy, dark, so all the people were out on the deck as much as possible, sharing food, talking, laughing, playing music. Some of the other passengers were playing accordions and fiddles and I began to dance in the middle of the deck. I danced and danced and all the people around me were laughing and clapping and watching me as I spun round and round in my short skirts. It was the happiest moment of my life!"*

My children will be born in California. It's not strange anymore, in this part of the world, in this time, to be born a thousand miles from the birthplace of your mother. My children will hear stories about the coquís and coffee flowers, about hurricanes and roosters crowing in the night, and will dig among old photographs to understand the homesick sadness that sometimes swallows me. Living among these dry golden hills, they will hear about rain falling for months, every afternoon at two o'clock, and someday I'll take them there, to the farm on the top of Indiera, redolent of my childhood, where they can play, irreverent, in the ruins of my house. Perhaps they will lie in bed among the sounds of the rainforest, and it will be the smell of eucalyptus that calls to them in their dreams.

Hace Tiempo

I grew up in apartments. This was the first house I lived in and what's more, I owned it. Well, Dick and I owned it, even though we bought it with his money. He had a bit of money. His inheritance, we called it. His father, Reuben, had died when Dick was sixteen, and his mother had inherited their house in Brooklyn and the money that Rube had killed himself making. When the spirit moved her, Ruth would part with some. But the fiction was that it was the "boys' money."

The rain on the roof, pit pat pat, just those first drops before the storm. How loud they are. I can hear each separate drop hit the tin roof like a pebble falling.

It's too soon for rain. Lord, if it starts raining this early in the day, I'll die asphyxiated. That's what it feels like, the shutters closed to keep out the water. Dark all day, darker if the lights fail, the small glow of a candle in the gloom of these brown wooden walls—at two in the afternoon. The air as wet as a saturated sponge: it would leak water if you poked your finger at it. And my clothes, I can't stand my clothes anymore. Clammy: cold and always a bit moist. Ugh.

I daydream fireplaces and the hot tropical sun my friends back home fantasize for me, hot tubs followed by big towels and freshly ironed sheets, and even underwear creased from the iron. All things warm and dry.

Yesterday I saw some dirt between my toes and I panicked. For a minute I was sure I was growing fungus. I could see it clearly, green and tendrily, taking over my feet, my back mildewed into a polka dot pattern.

I don't want to get up. Dick's back is hot. He's sending out heat like a furnace. I move closer, put my upper arm over his ribs, slip my other arm under my pillow, and close my eyes.

The sky has fallen! Avalanches of pebbles assault the roof. A million drums make music over my head. I fall asleep.

I remember where we were when we made up our minds to go to Puerto Rico. On a bench in a little park in front of a church in Ithaca, New York. All our more important moments took place on park benches.

It was evening and we were deciding our future. It was definitely time to decide. I was not getting what I wanted at Cornell, and Dick was graduating and had been told in his department that they had taught him all they knew and he should go to graduate school somewhere else. But where? In any case, there were more urgent things on our minds beside school. We were communists, though not too many people outside the FBI and CIA knew about it, and the U.S. Army was busy fighting communism in Korea and, we imagined, would soon ask Dick to help them out.

Just for a moment now I was back there, feeling it, the fear that we had no future, that Dick could be hauled off to jail any day for refusing to fight, that either of us might be arrested and jailed or concentration-camped for being communist. I'd been away from my overprotecting home and married for a year, a communist for two years. Before that we'd sat on another park bench and pledged to cleave to one another for eighty-eight years, exactly, and here we were wondering about the months ahead.

So before any of the things we feared could happen we would go to Puerto Rico. See it. It was my country, sort of. Dick wanted to know it, and I didn't much mind finding out about it and showing him. I'd grown up thinking of it as a kind of paradise, all palm trees, banana plants, sun, and warm breezes. We would go! We did.

God, I hate the smell of kerosene. It gets over everything, penetrates and never comes out again. Even my skin smells of it. And the flame makes such a greasy soot on the bottoms of my pots. It takes forever to get off and then it's on the cloths and washbasin so I have to scrub them off too.

The cheese melting on the macaroni smells O.K., even though I'm getting tired of it. Wonder what I can do to make it taste different. There's so little in the house.

"¿Señora?"

It's the little girl from next door. Her head just reaches over the bottom half of the Dutch door, and her eyes travel from the oilclothed counter to shelf to pots to wall to floor to me, picking up and storing details. I feel large and lumpish and out of place. I wish she wouldn't stare so.

"¿Si? ¿Que quieres?"

I sound so brusque. I don't know what to say, how to sound polite in Spanish. I recover a phrase.

"¿En que le puedo ayudar?"

Lord, now I sound formal, as if I were at a reception or something. She doesn't stop her survey of the room or me and takes in my jeans, my sweater, my breasts without the modest brasiel over them, my hair tied in a pony tail. Her words come out in a long swift stream.

"Mami mandó esto' huevo' que la' gallina' e'tan poniendo y pide perdon pol no venir ella mi'ma que no se siente bien pue' tiene un frio en el e'tomago y que si puedo bu'cal yerba buena en la finca que hay un pedazo detra' de la casa."

Yerba buena. Some sort of herb to cure something like a cold in the stomach? I think so. God knows what's really wrong with her. Well, I take the eggs and thank her, tell her to thank her mother very much and yes, she can pick all the yerba buena she wants. I wonder if it's the mint. I think it must be, and I bet I know which chickens laid the eggs, the ones that are always here scratching at the newly planted beds eating up our seed. I might as well get some nourishment out of them.

"Gracias, señora." but she hangs on to the door and peers in, watches me turn the macaroni off, watches me move things around from here to there and back again. I wait for her to go. My back hurts where her eyes are poking into it. I can't stand it any more.

"Perdóname." I slowly push the door open, step out, shut it firmly behind me, and walk away to the privy where I can shut the door in her face without shame. She turns and skips away up the hill toward the mint patch to my relief, to my boundless relief.

We found a farm in the coffee region where the economy had been depressed for sixty years and prices were low. This land had not grown coffee since San Felipe, the big hurricane of 1928. The piece we bought held the remains of the center of operations of a large prosperous plantation: cisterns that gathered water for washing the berries; a glacis, a large cement platform for drying the hulled seed, buried foundations, crumbling steps leading from terrace to terrace. We moved into the board house built on stilts, room added to small room over thirty years. The rooms with the hand-hewn floor boards had survived that old storm. We put our bed in the larger of the two.

It's a great day for laundry. It's bright and sunny and smells so good, of grass smells and coffee roasting in one of the neighboring houses. Maybe doña Sica's, where early this morning I heard the pounding of the big pestle in the oversized pilón, hulling the coffee beans: pound, pound, pound. I woke to it and to church bells ringing down the hill, cocks crowing, and Mercedes' children going to get water at the spring.

I took Dick his breakfast. He still can't get out of bed except to go to the privy and he comes back white, as if the hepatitis had bleached him, not yellowed him. I'm leaving the dishes because I'm washing clothes today. It's a wonderful day for drying: all sun and breezes. The morning chill is still in the air but it will soon be gone. In the meantime I'll wear Dick's flannel shirt, the green and brown plaid. It's comfortable over my belly which sticks way out in front of me. I'm proud of it. It's mine, it's large, I'm large! I've gained a lot of weight, and for the first time in my life I'm fat, my face round as the moon, as the sunflowers by the side of the house. I'm happy. It's funny how happy I am even with Dick sick in bed, with the farm not paying, no money for vitamins or maternity clothes.

I'm even happy about things like doing the laundry in this old tub. The water is so shiny wet, the day so clear and sunny, and Dick is in the bedroom for me to go and talk to and kiss whenever I feel like, and I'm big as a balloon, as an elephant. The baby turns over inside me, a small revolution. I see its fists and knees and elbows jut out suddenly from beside my belly button like a cat under the covers, a bulge that disappears then reappears in a second somewhere else.

Now for the tub. Lord, it's awkward getting it up on the box outside. I'm heating water on the back porch. That used to be the kitchen for the people that lived here before. I prefer cooking on a kerosene stove in the house—I've turned a small room on the north side into a kitchen—but I use the wood fire on the high cement table for heating water for baths and washing clothes.

I fill the bucket from the rusty rain barrel and balance it on the rocks on the table. I've sprinkled kerosene on the wood between the rocks. All I need to do is set a match to it to start it. But I have to fan it with a piece of cardboard box to make sure it will keep burning.

I've got the sheet and some underwear soaking in soapy water so I can go find out what Sukita is doing among the sunflowers. She seemed to be hunting. She pounced on something but it was Marietta she was stalking, and they're rolling around in the earth like kittens.

The sunflowers are so tall, bright, and round-faced. I've never grown flowers before except for five straggly morning glories in a sixth-story window box. I love sunflowers—and geraniums, too. I wonder if mine will ever get like the ones by the rectory. They're bushes, three feet tall, long-limbed and red-flowered.

The carnation seedlings are almost big enough to transplant. I plan to give some to doña Sica and Mercedes. They've been so good about sharing their plants, and it's the nicest gift you can give a woman around here—a plant, or a cutting—un ganchito. "¿Me puede regalar un ganchito?" It's the plants that make me feel part of the neighborhood, the line of soil-filled planted cans—juice cans, coffee cans—on the porch rail. My plants. My house. My neighborhood.

It's 1955. I'm pregnant again. I'd miscarried one, and I nearly lost this child. I'm thin all over except for my belly. César and Jane live up the hill. Dick and I plan, tentatively, for Dick to go to the states for graduate study for a year and for me to stay on the farm. I have this dream. I'm scared of the dream. Even now.

They have her, the Nazis. A big stout woman in a Nazi uniform stands over my little daughter strapped to a chair, and they have the top of her skull off. You can see the surface of her brain all indented and convoluted and greyish white except for the ditches which are dark and grey, and it's her moist living pulsing delicate brain and it's out there, uncovered. They're going to poke things into it! How can I stop them from doing this to my little girl? How did I let this happen? She's so small and vulnerable and she's in their hands and I am helpless and how can I stop them?

I'm so heavy, so tired, so sleepy. It feels like a dense fog descending on me, a coastal fog. Not like the breath of clouds that rush over the mountain and through the house on foggy days, but a dense heavy feeling that starts at the top of my head, weights my eyelids down, slows my arms, and when it hits my legs, I have to lie down. So I rush to lock the gate, the door, to put toys out for Lori to keep her busy because now I must lie down before it blankets me, before I fall.

When I come out, emerge from my stupor, I can't see her and I panic. I feel my heart pierce through my ribs in fear. Then I hear her babble. She's O.K. There she is. Whatever does she find to occupy her down that hole? It's the knot hole in the flooring by the door to the kitchen, and she often lies down with her eye glued to it talking and singing to herself. I hear chickens under the house. She must be watching them.

"Aurorita! Come! Did you miss me?" I sit down by her. "How about a hug? A big girl-squeezing hug? Umm!"

It's hard getting up. I would like to sit here for a while at child level, at child responsibility, and have someone bring me toys and books, hug me, wash my face, lead me to the table, and set food before me.

"Ugh. I can't believe how slow I feel. I can't believe I used to feel so full of life and energy carrying Lori. I hate feeling tired all the time. There's so much to do and so little to do it with.

Last week I went up to Jane's to take a shower. She has hot running water. Besides, I hardly fit in the washtub anymore. Once I get in there's not much room for water. What a sight. All that belly and me wrapped around it, and the old zinc-lined washtub wrapped around me, with a thin stream of rapidly cooling water spread between me and the tub like oil so I can slip out of it again.

I don't want to go back up there again though, even if it's lovely having all that hot water on my skin. In the hospital delivering Lori I startled the nurses by getting under a hot shower and staying there till I was red like the rectory geraniums. But in Jane's bathroom there is a mirror hanging high in the wall and tilted down so you can see your whole self and I did. I saw my body completely for the first time in months, and there it was, that long pointy belly and right above it my ribs, like bony fingers gripping my chest, my arms cadaverously thin, my sticklike legs. I looked and cried, tears wetting my face and dropping, plop, on the terrace of my belly.

I stood there for a long while. God, I was scared! I looked like a picture taken in famine country, one of those you look at in a book and shudder. I would rather freeze in my tin tub than face myself again. I wish Dick were here. I need a hug.

I've got to fatten up. How, I don't know. I don't feel like eating most of the time. At least I'm not throwing up any more. And I'm not losing weight.

What shall I do? For lunch, I mean. Rice for supper. Not macaroni and cheese, please! What I want is green bananas and potatoes and sliced onion. . . no, no raw onion, I'll taste it for hours. But I'll make a verdura anyway. Mercedes gave me some yautía yesterday and Lori will eat that with a boiled egg, so I can put together that concoction of boiled bananas, roots, eggs, salad, and olive oil that tastes of childhood. Next best thing to getting taken care of.

There are still green bananas at the top of the bunch hung in the kitchen. The lower ones are ripe, the middle ones are green tinged with yellow but the upper ones are green as green. They're easier to peel than plátanos and even green like this they carry a sweetness, a promise of the candy sticks they will become. But oh I miss plátano, so hard, so green, tasting only of itself. They're scarce out here.

I need to talk about how I miss them. It's now or never. No one will refuse me anything by way of food while I'm pregnant. The sacredness of the antojo! I don't even have to say I'm antojá for plátano. I just have to talk about how I miss it. When I go to the store with Lori after her nap I'll try it on don Paco. He always has a few plantain plants on his farm. Who knows, I may have plátano for my verdura this week yet.

But now I must get to work. To the sounds of the chickens under the house, of Lori talking to herself, I dip out the water and set it to boil, slit the green skin off the banana, use the knife to pry it off, slide it into the boiling water con un poquito de sal. Put the hairy root in the wash basin and pare the skin off and rinse and pare and rinse, keeping the slimy cream-colored surface of the yautía clean, watching the purple threads on it emerge under the knife, feeling the peeled root slither under my fingers. Cut it. Pop it in the water. Turn down the flame.

Twenty minutes. I push open the lower half of the door and sit on the step in the warm sun, watch Lori play with sticks in the dirt, and wait.

Kitchens

I went into the kitchen just now to stir the black beans and rice, the shiny black beans floating over the smooth brown grains of rice and the zucchini turning black, too, in the ink of the beans. Mine is a California kitchen, full of fresh vegetables and whole grains, bottled spring water and yogurt in plastic pints, but when I lift the lid from that big black pot, my kitchen fills with the hands of women who came before me, washing rice, washing beans, picking through them so deftly, so swiftly, that I could never see what the defects were in the beans they threw quickly over one shoulder out the window. Some instinct of the fingertips after years of sorting to feel the rottenness of the bean with a worm in it or a chewed-out side. Standing here, I see the smooth red and brown and white and speckled beans sliding through their fingers into bowls of water, the gentle clicking rush of them being poured into the pot, hear the hiss of escaping steam, smell the bean scum floating on the surface under the lid. I see grains of rice settling in a basin on the counter, turning the water milky with rice polish and the talc they use to make the grains so smooth; fingers dipping, swimming through the murky white water, feeling for the grain with the blackened tip, the brown stain.

From the corner of my eye, I see the knife blade flashing, reducing mounds of onions, garlic, cilantro, and green peppers into sofrito to be fried up and stored, and best of all is the pound and circular grind of the pilón: *pound, pound, thump, grind, pound, pound, thump, grind. Pound, pound* (the garlic and oregano mashed together), *THUMP!* (the mortar lifted and slammed down to loosen the crushed herbs and spices from the wooden bowl), *grind* (the slow rotation of the pestle smashing the oozing mash around and around, blending the juices, the green stain of cilantro and oregano, the sticky yellowing garlic, the grit of black pepper).

It's the dance of the cocinera: to step outside
fetch the bucket of water, turn,
all muscular grace and striving,
pour the water, light dancing in the pot,
and set the pail down on the blackened wood.
The blue flame glitters in its dark corner,
and coffee steams in the small white pan.
Gnarled fingers, mondando ajo,
picando cebolla, cortando pan,
colando café,
stirring the rice with a big long spoon
filling ten bellies
out of one soot-black pot.

It's a magic, a power, a ritual of love and work that rises up in my
kitchen, thousands of miles from those women in cotton dresses who
twenty years ago taught the rules of its observance to me, the ap-
prentice, the novice, the girl-child: "Don't go out without wrapping
your head, child, you've been roasting coffee, y te va' a pa'mar!" "This
much coffee in the colador, girl, or you'll be serving brown water."
"Dip the basin in the river, so, to leave the mud behind." "Always
peel the green bananas under cold water, mijita, or you'll cut your
fingers and get mancha on yourself and the stain never comes out:
that black sap stain of guineo verde and plátano, the stain that marks
you forever."

So I peel my bananas under running water from the faucet, but the
stain won't come out, and the subtle earthy green smell of that sap
follows me, down from the mountains, into the cities, to places where
banana groves are like a green dream, unimaginable by daylight: Chicago, New Hampshire, Oakland. So I travel miles on the bus to the immigrant markets of other people, coming home laden with bundles,
and even, now and then, on the plastic frilled tables of the supermarket, I find a small curved green bunch to rush home, quick, before it ripens, to peel and boil, bathing in the scent of its cooking,

bringing the river to flow through my own kitchen now, the river of my place on earth, the green and musty river of my grandmothers, dripping, trickling, tumbling down from the mountain kitchens of my people.

Sugar Poem

Poetry
is something refined
in your vocabulary,
taking its place at the table
in a silver bowl: essence
of culture.

I come from the earth
where the cane was grown.
I know
the knobbed rooting,
green spears, heights of
caña
against the sky,
purple plumed.
I know the backache
of the machetero,
the arc of steel
cutting, cutting,
the rhythm of harvest
leaving acres of sharp spikes
that wound the feet—
and the sweet smoke
of the llamarada:
rings of red fire burning
dark sugar into the wind.

My poems grow from the ground.
I know what they are made of:
heavy, raw and green.

Sugar,
you say, is sweet.
One teaspoon in a cup of coffee...
life's not so bad.

Caña, I reply,
yields many things:
molasses
for the horses,
rum for the tiredness
of the machetero,
industrial
alcohol to cleanse,
distill, to burn
as fuel.

I don't write my poems
for anybody's sweet tooth.

My poems are acetylene torches
welding steel.
My poems are flamethrowers
cutting paths through the world.
My poems are bamboo spears
opening the air.
They come from the earth,
common and brown.

1930

My grandmother Lola, with her beautiful sagging face and her fine, black and silver hair, sits on the bed weeping as she tells me the story, tears and words spilling slowly. She loves the weeping and telling and the gestures she incorporates, rolling her eyes to heaven, casting them down. But the story is nonetheless true, and I don't move, so as not to break the thread.

The images, once heard, are unforgettable. My abuelo walking ninety blocks to look for work, saving the nickel so he could take the trolley home. The janitor's job opening up just in time, mijita. There was a group of Puerto Ricans, tú sabes, people who all knew each other and looked out for each other, not familia, but parecido, because, you know, there weren't so many of us in New York then. They said, "Who should get this job?" and someone said, "Manolin, because he has a new baby." So they sent for him and took him down there at night and taught him how to use the vacuum cleaner, one of those big industrial ones, and the next day he got the job. As soon as they paid him, he went straight to the store and bought food. We hadn't eaten in three days. Imagínate!, with Sari nursing. She was taking all that milk out and nothing was going in. I was así (she holds up her pinkie to show me how thin and laughs), así. He brought home a couple of eggs and a little butter. He had to cook them for me because I was too weak to get up, and then he fed them to me because I couldn't even hold the spoon. Sari and I just lay on the bed together. She'd be drinking the milk and I'd be just lying there, too weak to move. And she heaves a deep quavering sigh, absent-mindedly scratching the skin of my bare leg.

There is a memory of hunger in me, a hunger from before birth that aches in the hollows of my fingers, my hands, my arms, bones caving in on themselves from hunger, stomach swelling, teeth falling out. My mother is there, too, tiny and dark-haired and black-eyed, her mouth sucking and sucking.

This is a story I make up from the scraps my mother and grandmother have let fall, a story I tell myself over and over, embroidering it, filling in the missing details of wind and weather and smells, of how my grandfather's hands clutch at the coat against the cold, how he leans forward into the wind like a steamboat; the way my grandmother's face is drawn and thin, the dim light of the bedroom where she lay, and the sharp urgency of my mother's cries; the smell of those eggs cooking and how they felt in Lola's stomach, those first few bites. My mother is the infant in the picture, but this is not my mother's story. It is my story for her, told to myself as I invent the details of her history, the foundations of my own. I lean on my grandmother's bed in the heat and humidity of Bayamon in summer, gathering material.

"I had a brown dress," she says after a moment. "That's all I had to wear. Sí, mija! One dress. When I had to wash it, I took it off and wore my slip until it was dry. We called it 'wash and wear.'" She laughs again, that snorting laugh of my grandmother's that I love so much, the one that erupts into the middle of her best dramas. "I'll never forget that brown dress."

And I think of my mother loving brown, the rich, comforting earthy warmth of that color which was the only one her mother wore during the first year of Sari's life; and I think of Lola's closet now, packed to the point of explosion with clothing of brilliant colors mixed wildly, a tropical rainbow of rayon and cotton and polyester blends: knit pants and cotton housedresses and silky negligees and satiny synthetic blouses, never again just one brown dress.

There is this picture: my thin grandmother with her suckling child lying half starved together on a bed in a dark old tenement building. There is also another picture: long-limbed and graceful as a young stork, radiant with life, she stands on the roof with neighbors and cousins, her place near the sky. We look at it in silence, then, "I always wanted to sing," she says. "I used to pray that I would wake up able to sing. I always had this crooked little squeaky voice. Las nenas se burlaban de mí. But if I could wake up one morning singing, I would die happy."

Class Poem

This is my poem in celebration of my middle class privilege
This is my poem to say out loud
I'm glad I had food, and shelter, and shoes,
glad I had books and travel, glad there was air and light
and room for poetry.

This poem is for Tita, my best friend
who played in the dirt with me
and married at eighteen (which was late) and who was a scientist
but instead she bore six children   and four of them died
Who wanted to know the exact location of color
in the hibiscus petal, and patiently peeled away the thinnest,
most translucent layers to find it
and who works in a douche bag factory in Maricao.

This poem is for the hunger of my mother
discovering books at thirteen in the New York Public Library
who taught me to read when I was five
and when we lived on a coffee farm
subscribed to a mail-order library,
who read the Blackwell's catalogue
like a menu of delights
and when we moved from Puerto Rico to the States
we packed 100 boxes of books and 40 of everything else.

This poem is for my father's immigrant Jewish family.
For my great-grandfather Abe Sackman
who worked in Bridgeport making nurse's uniforms
and came home only on weekends, for years, and who painted
on bits of old wooden crates, with housepaint,
birds and flowers for his great-grandchildren
and scenes of his old-country childhood.

This poem celebrates my father the scientist
who left the microscope within reach,
with whom I discovered the pomegranate eye of the fruitfly,
and yes, the exact location of color in a leaf.

This poem celebrates my brother the artist
who began to draw when he was two,
and so my parents bought him reams of paper
and when he used them up, bought him more,
and today it's a silkscreen workshop
and posters that travel around the world,
and I'm glad for him   and for Pop with his housepaints
and Tita staining the cement with crushed flowers
searching for color
and my mother shutting out the cries of her first-born
ten minutes at a time
to sketch the roofs and elevated tracks
in red-brown pastels.

This is for Norma
who died of parasites in her stomach when she was four
I remember because her mother wailed her name
screaming and sobbing
one whole afternoon in the road in front of our school
and for Angélica
who caught on fire while stealing kerosene for her family
and died in pain
because the hospital she was finally taken to
knew she was poor
and would not give her the oxygen she needed to live
but wrapped her in greased sheets
so that she suffocated.

This is a poem against the wrapped sheets,
against guilt.

This is a poem to say:
my choosing to suffer gives nothing
to Tita and Norma and Angélica
and that not to use the tongue, the self-confidence, the training
my privilege bought me
is to die again for people who are already dead
and who wanted to live.

And in case anyone here confuses the paraphernalia
with the thing itself
let me add that I lived with rats and termites
no carpet   no stereo   no TV
that the bath came in buckets and was heated on the stove
that I read by kerosene lamp and had Sears mail-order clothes
and that that has nothing to do
with the fact of my privilege.

Understand, I know exactly what I got: protection and choice
and I am through apologizing.
I am going to strip apology from my voice
my posture
my apartment
my clothing
my dreams
because the voice that says the only true puertorican
is a dead or dying puertorican
is the enemy's voice—
the voice that says
"How can you let yourself shine when Tita, when millions
are daily suffocating in those greased sheets..."
I refuse to join them there.
I will not suffocate.
I will not hold back.
Yes, I had books and food and shelter and medicine
and I intend to survive.

The
Meeting
Of
So
Many
Roads

Child Of The Americas

I am a child of the Americas,
a light-skinned mestiza of the Caribbean,
a child of many diaspora, born into this continent at a crossroads.

I am a U.S. Puerto Rican Jew,
a product of the ghettos of New York I have never known.
An immigrant and the daughter and granddaughter of immigrants.
I speak English with passion: it's the tongue of my consciousness,
a flashing knife blade of crystal, my tool, my craft.

I am Caribeña, island grown. Spanish is in my flesh,
ripples from my tongue, lodges in my hips:
the language of garlic and mangoes,
the singing in my poetry, the flying gestures of my hands.
I am of Latinoamerica, rooted in the history of my continent:
I speak from that body.

I am not african. Africa is in me, but I cannot return.
I am not taína. Taíno is in me, but there is no way back.
I am not european. Europe lives in me, but I have no home there.

I am new. History made me. My first language was spanglish.
I was born at the crossroads
and I am whole.

The Dinner

Perhaps you have seen The Dinner Party, tables set with linens and fine tableware. Dinner, in the dining room, decorous.

I didn't go. My folks didn't either, not my womenfolks. They don't go to things like that, weren't invited, wouldn't know what to say or do, how to eat. Besides, the food is boring.

My womenfolks are giving their own party. In the kitchen. First names only, or m'hija, negra, ne, honey, sugah, dear. The table is scrubbed and each plate and bowl is different, wood, clay, papier mâché, metal, basketry, a leaf, a coconut shell. Each is painted, carved by a woman.

The table has a cloth woven by one, dyed by another, embroidered by another still. It's too small for the table but is put there in the center every year in memory of our mothers. We prepare the meal with our own particular tools. Squatting by the doorsill she pounds garlic and herbs. And *she* chops with a cleaver—garlic, ginger, scallions, peppers—parts a small piece of beef into a thousand slices. Someone toasts coffee, someone else grinds bananas for banana beer. Two are washing rice. One is cleaning a fish, trying pork fat, peeling plantains, scrubbing yams, chopping hot peppers. The air is rich with smells and sounds.

Each wears her colors for feasting: red, orange, green, turquoise, blue, yellow, gold flashes as she moves, stoops, reaches, twists, stirs, turns, opens, closes. We will eat where we can sit, on stools, on the floor, lean against the wall, squat, stand, with what we have, with sticks, fingers, a shared spoon, a piece of shell.

This is the dinner. We don't know our forbears' names with a certainty. They aren't written anywhere. We honor them because they have kept it all going, all the civilizations erected on their backs, all the dinner parties given with their labor. And they gave us life, kept us going, brought us to where we are.

Come! Lay that dishcloth down. Eat, dear, eat. There will be time later, and hands enough, for the cleaning.

South

Flying south, south, into the deepest south, there was the feeling of being pulled farther home than I've ever been. I began to wonder if the body does have its secret reservoirs of memory after all, cubbyholes in the cells, that pass on from generation to generation the smell of a place once loved, the feel of its air on the skin. Flying in the dark over Mexican desert and then later over the sea, my heart sang back to the heart of my continent, singing in the night, calling me, pulling me near.

First we crossed the high thundery places. Too dark, too cloudy to say for certain, "that was a peak," but now and again, flashing between gulfs of black air and mountainous piles of moonlit cloud, between sideways-stabbing strokes of lightning I saw what was too white, too sharp to be cloud. Something cold and crisp and clear as a quena song. My head grew light and the man next to me said the oxygen was thin up here, climbing over the spine of the world. Then the thunder fell behind us, the perpetual growling of those wild uppermost Andes, and we coasted slowly down into the richest air of the beginning.

In the beginning my blood traveled from this air, and returns to it in my deepest dreams: where the trees all but shut out the sun, and in a green dimness where the jaguar runs like a vivid flame along the branches and ground, my people still walk, still hunt, still stand mouth open, laughing up into the rain.

Taíno, Aruaca, Gauraní. I follow the thread of my blood back from the cave I once found in the hills near my home: the pottery shard, the painted wall, I follow it, bright and tremulous out of the coded messages of my bones, the archeology of my flesh. The Díaz clan coming down out of the hills to intermarry, carrying the precious drop that is mine, as they carried precious water in gourds and skin sacks on the long voyage (I remember it) out of the forests of the Orinoco, over the mountains and nearly to the edge of breathable air, then down to the swampy coast, a millenium ago perhaps, and up the chain of islands, a journey of many generations, of hundreds of years, never spilling it, never leaving it behind.

To the villages in the coastal valleys of my island, netting fish from the sea, growing manioc, yuca, achiote, making palm wine, weaving hamacas, painting their faces red and black: seed juice and sap, dipping arrows against their marauding cousins the Caribs. How they journeyed from beach to beach until they came here, to Boriquén, Island of Crabs, and caught the crabs and roasted them, and roasted a jutía with achiote and wild onions, and feasted right there on the beach.

I feast with them and remember the time of copper and blood when the Spaniards came and you thought they must eat gold, they were so desperate for it, and you blew on the conch and rose up and fought them, and then the war was over and you said "jíbaro" meaning one who runs away to be free, and a small band of you fled up into the mountains I was born in, to Indiera, "place of the Indians."

Still you said guaraguao for hawk, guamá for the sticky sweet pod, guayaba for the small round yellow fruit, words sweet and round in the mouth that traveled with you from the place of many rivers, where you were a people of the Guaraní people, and life was wet and growing and you hunted for weeks at a time under the endless green shadows.

The shadows are not endless anymore. Each day the bulldozers bite out another piece of the jungle and the sun invades the green world and little rivers dry up in their beds and the fish die in the mud. But all night long one night, I flew above it, with not a single light below me. Nothing but the murmuring of a million rivers and a hundred million new leaves opening and breathing into the night . . . and myself, a late leaf of that ancient tree, opening and breathing a rich and heady oxygen out of my deepest root.

Africa

Africa waters the roots of my tree,
    pulses in my sap,
    seeps thru my heartwood.
Though my roots reach into the soils of two Americas,
Africa waters my tree.

The Other Heritage

*for June Jordan and Teish and all other Black
women at the San Francisco Poetry Workshop,
January 1980*

I forgot   I forgot the other heritage   the other strain   refrain
    the silver thread thru my sound   the ebony sheen to my life
    to the look of things to the sound of how I grew up which was
in Harlem right down in Spanish Harlem El Barrio and bounded
I always say to foreigners from Minnesota Ohio and Illinois bounded on the North by Italians and on the South by Black Harlem
A library in each of these almost forbidden places so no wonder
I didn't take off with books till I hit the South Bronx   What I didn't
forget was the look of Ithaca Rochester Minneapolis and Salt Lake
    bleached   bleeded and bleached   the street full of white
ghosts like Chinese visions   And the first time Dick and I drove
back thru New York past Amsterdam Avenue right thru the heart
of Harlem I breathed again   safe   brown and black walking the
streets   safe   My mami taught me   my teacher taught
me   everybody taught me   watch out   black   smelly   savage
keep out of the way   I did too   so how come I come to feel
    safe   when I hit Harlem   when I hit a city with enough color
    when a city gets moved in on   when Main Street Vermont looks
mottled   agouti   black and brown and white   when the sounds
of the english Black folk speak and the sounds of Spanish wiggle
thru the clean lit air   I still shy and start from Black men from
about thirteen on but then I shy and start from all men starting from
when they think to be men and so do the things men do   my mami
taught me that and that stuck   but then I learnt that on my own
too   I got myself a clean clear sense of danger   that's what
smells   not black skin   but danger stalking the streets for me   I
can smell it a mile away wafting to me in the breeze   I keep down-
wind   raise my head to sniff the air   I only muse and rest my
neck when in the herd and in the day and loping thru people traffic

on the streets surrounded by the sounds of wheeled traffic in the
streets   I think and plan and forget to look but not alone and not
at nite   I lift my head   I sniff   I smell the danger and wheel
and run long before he thinks   maybe   she looks about right
a morsel for my appetite   I bound away and pant   safe   for
this time safe   but all I feel when I sit down with you Black
woman   the only danger in my air is from some whirring voice
inside that always says   you don't belong   and if you don't utter
just just right they will know you don't belong and toss you out   and
I feel that every time with every group of any color no matter what
they speak   but what I feel inside nowhere near that grating prat-
ing voice is   well O.K.!   this sounds just right   this here music
is music to my ears here   I hear something that feels like   oh
like Carlos Gardel moaning his tangos   like the special beat caribbean drums do   I forgot this heritage   african Black up here in
this cold place   the sound of african in english   of drums in these
musics   I forgot I breathed you with my air and declared
fine   and when you're not there I look and ask for where you've
gone   but I know   I know why I forgot   I'm not supposed to
remember   what I do remember is to walk in straight and white
into the store and say good morning in my see how white how
upper class refined and kind voice all crisp with consonants bristling
with syllables   protective coloring in racist fields looks white and
crisp like cabbage   looks tidy like laid-out gardens   like white
aprons on black dresses   like please and thank you and you're
welcome   like neat and clean and see I swept and scrubbed and
polished   ain't I nice   que hay de criticar   will I do   will I
pass   will you let me thru   will they let me be   not see me here
beneath my skin   behind my voice   crouched and quiet and so
so still   not see not hear me there where I crouch   hiding my
eyes   my indian bones   my spanish sounds   muttering
mielda   qué gente fría y féa   se creen gran cosa   ai!   escupe
chica en su carifresca   en su cariféa   méate ahi en el piso féo
y frío   yo valgo más que un piso limpio   yo valgo más   yo
valgo   cágate en l'alfombra chica   arráncale el pelo   yo quiero
salir de aqui   yo quiero salir de ti   yo quiero salir   you
see   she's me   she's the me says   safe   sarita   safe when

I see you many and Black around the table   behind me in the big
room and up in front   June Jordan   how you belt it out and
how I take it in right to where she sits brown and golden   and
when she and I laughed big last nite I was not "too loud"   I was
not "too much"   I was just right   just me   just brown and pink
and full of drums inside beating rhythm for my feet   my tongue
    my eyes   my hands   my arms swinging and smacking   I was
just right   just right   just right sépanlo niñas   m'hijas trigueñas
bellas   sépalo June Jordan   mujer feroz   aqui me quedo y aqui
estoy   right!

Tita's Poem

Oh, brown skinny girl with eyes like chips of mica
what did we know, straddling the flamboyan branch
hanging dreamy eyed, shivering, in the sun?
What did we know, squatting
over the swollen roots of hillside ginger
tipping our wild little animal hips
to catch the stream of water from a roof
right between the legs?
Nothing had a name then.

I remember a photograph in Ladies Home Journal
two women, skinny, stringy haired, gaunt eyed:
"Lesbian Junkie Prostitutes in Jail" said the caption
I never connected that word with us   still
I remembered the picture.
Kiss my mouth you said, and wondered if you'd get pregnant
and said you didn't care.

What did we know that we don't know now?
When I come back, I grieved, you'll be married, with babies
and you said *no, no, espera pa' que tu veas, verás que no.*
All that last spring we gathered orchids deep in the rainforest
bringing them to our garden,
binding them to the wood with black thread:
green, fresh flowers never meant for the sun,
bouquets of dawn never touched
by the careless brutal burning of noon.

In the years since then you've spilled children from you
like wasted blood
half of them dying before you could learn their names.
Still, I imagine you, thin and dear,
gnawing at the rinds of green guavas,
tasting each orange to see if it was bitter
or sweet, your dark head bent to my breast.

If I were to find you now, with your thieving husband and three
surviving children   if I were to come to you now in some dark
and stuffy, overcrowded living room in New York
where photographs of your wedding and nieces and nephews
crowd the end tables
you sitting on the plastic-covered couch,
with the inner stillness of a girl still moving
in the shadows of trees
If I were to come to you now and take you   thin
into my arms   would you remember me
and be wild and daring again, reaching up into the sky
to pluck the sun?

Coffee Bloom

In my country
the coffee blooms between hurricanes
fragile white blossoms that a raindrop could trample into the mud
a delicacy of lace
a hoax of helplessness smothering up the wiry wood within.

On the hillside, deep in the rainforest
is a bush gone wild fifty years ago
its root as thick as my arm.
Here in the green shadows we whisper, the bush and I, our secret,
that hidden root
the reason we don't tremble, though the bruised petals flail
no matter how wildly the wet wind blows.

Concepts Of Pollution

That's what they were interested in—concepts of pollution, rituals of liminality, structures of myth. Not air pollution or water pollution, but more like *kosher* and *tref*, you know, mixing meat with milk. And here is Yalman in Inman Square polluting it like all hell. Christ! What's he doing here? He belongs in Hyde Park, where the effluvium of the University of Chicago runs through the streets in dirty streams, where you know you can't walk without high boots around your soul to protect it. But here I am on my way to Schlesinger Library to read about what makes women angry, bare-souled and sunnily smiling, and POW, Yalman, professor of anthropology first class, master of concept and abstraction, polluting my neighborhood. Come Rosario, this is the outer frill of Harvard and such as he belong at Harvard dispensing airy principles and lifting their cuffs daintily above teeming reality.

Now what have we learned about *my* concepts of pollution? Oh, drop it! Let's be real, not anthropological. I can't bear to see him because I want to forget the whole thing, leave it all behind. And I can't, and not just because the Yalmans of the world travel to Harvard and appear in Inman Square, but because the boots didn't protect my soul, and it is seared and stained and I am angry. "What makes women angry?" I asked myself as I set out to Schlesinger Library. And on the way I met Yalman and this is what made me angry: concepts of pollution.

We studied concepts of pollution and marriage customs and puberty rites, and no one mentioned rape: the fact of it or the pain of it, of what it means to be a little girl of eight and be married and be raped. Or to be a woman cast out into the streets and stoned because the way you've loved pollutes the caste, or be locked up day after day and be screamed at and hated and feared because you threaten to pollute the caste.

We studied the structures of myth. Do you know Levi-Strauss wrote an essay on the pregnant-boy myths of the Pawnee Indians, myths about how some boys got supernatural help to become doctors—so-called medicine men—without a word about doctoring among the Pawnees in the 1800s, without a word about the desperate hopelessness of it with people dying of all the diseases of starvation, the hungry, cold, winters, and the attacks of the Sioux? How the men, and men they were, who collected these stories and wrote them down, went among hundreds of Pawnees where once there were thousands, and how families inherited doctor's kits—"medicine bundles"—from dead doctors and no longer knew what the pieces were for—the feathers, the herbs, the skins—because they, the doctors, had died before passing it on, before they could teach their skills to others.

Do you know Levi-Strauss wrote an essay on the Caduveo, about how these South American people covered their faces and bodies in painted designs in red and black? Do you know he decided they were exactly like people in a medieval court, in leather and feathers with their dependent serfs and nobles, so aristocratic they wouldn't mingle even with Europeans, that they were like the court cards of the human deck with their painted kings and painted queens? Do you know that the missionaries wondered, and he wondered, how these people could cover up god's good body with tattooed designs and patterns in genipapo juice, that they decided that the Caduveo were arrogant enough to despise god and nature, that they murdered their young and practiced abortion. And Levi-Strauss compliments the Jesuit priest who wrote ten chapters on the vices of the Caduveo, fulminated on their unchristian degeneracy. Do you know that, finally, this exalted anthropologist believed that the Caduveo were so wrapped up in their Alice-in-Wonderland importance that they practically disappeared—just 200, ragged and beggarly in the 1930s, and only themselves to blame.

And not a word about their homes and lands and lives being smack in the path that the greedy Spanish and Portuguese had mapped out as their way to the gold of the Incas, not a word about how they were despised and killed, infected and killed, tricked and killed, poisoned and killed.

And I was there to be a scholar, there to be an anthropologist. Not there to be a person, a woman. Not there to care that I was Puerto Rican, a child of Taino Indians, of Spaniards, of African slaves. Not there to question, to argue. Not there to identify. Not there to cry. Certainly not there to cry.

No wonder I drank. I've never written these words before in sober daylight. I'd scribble incomprehensibly, drunkenly, in large penciled letters on pads of paper or in small script on little strips which I would find in the morning. I'd write after staying up drinking, talking to myself in the mirror, shouting angrily at Yalman, Turner, Schneider, at Levi-Strauss and Malinowski. Then I would write about Pawnees dying in the thin winter sunlight, coughing up blood, or Polynesians dying on the beach in the Pacific, shot by passing whalers, or Caduveo dying of Spanish gunshot. I wrote about Wounded Knee and Canyon de Chelly, places I had names for, and all the beaches and valleys and rocky plains in Africa, in Canada, in Australia, on the Pacific Islands, on the Caribbean Islands, in tropical South America, in Arctic North America, places for which I had no names. A soundless litany of death by exploration, of death by pacification, of death by manifest destiny, of death by pioneering and frontiering and private enterprising, of death by hard-working, god-fearing farming and gold-rushing, of death by capitalist expansion in the sixteenth, seventeenth, eighteenth, nineteenth, and twentieth centuries.

Let me tell you about the dolphin. The fish dolphin, as my biologist husband is quick to correct, not the mammal dolphin. When this fish is killed, pulled out of its life-giving water and asphyxiated in the life-denying air, it changes colors as it slowly chokes to death. I've never seen this fish. I read about it during the time when I was reading about concepts of pollution during the day and mourning the dying Pawnee at night. They say as it dies it turns beautiful colors, iridescent blue to electric green to dark purple to purple red. All over its body these colors pulse while we watch. Anthropologists watch murdered peoples die and look at the colors of their customs, the movements of the rigor mortis. And the emotional ones write vivid descriptions, the methodical ones take meticulous notes, the scientific ones make careful measurements. All the while the dolphin dies, the people writhe as their mothers die or their children or their friends, and we write and publish and get promoted, give or receive prizes and grants, and we never mention pain or sorrow or anger or death.

I tried. It's like describing the contents of an unflushed toilet at a garden party. That's what it all was: one prolonged tea party serving dying dolphin. It's no wonder I felt sick to my stomach all the while, that I was always angry, angry all the time while I smiled, while I wrote papers on Levi-Strauss and his playful toying with myths and rituals, with women's lives and women's kin, while I drank and drank and drank.

Drink deadens the pain, and now I don't drink and the pain returns undeadened, unalloyed, clear, and punishing. How can I bear it? How do you mourn endless numbers of people in endless numbers of places? Is there a form for it, a requisite time and place for mourning? Is there ever an end to it? Can there ever be an end to it?

I feel guilt for not shouting it out, for not screaming in their ears, not making endless scenes, burning their papers, their buildings. Bertolt Brecht said, "These are indeed terrible times when to talk of trees seems a kind of silence about injustice."

To talk about concepts of pollution is more than a kind of silence about injustice: It is a lie about murder. That's what anthropology is—your anthropology Turner and Levi-Strauss, your's University of Chicago, Harvard, Yale—a lie about murder, an intellectual necrology, a crime.

Distress Signals

(Reuters) Iki Island, Japan. About 4000 dolphins massed around this island today, forcing fishing boats back to port a day after fishermen from the island slashed and stabbed about 200 dolphins to death after trapping them in nets. Meanwhile, an American environmentalist was formally charged in Nagasaki with freeing some 250 dolphins that have been trapped in the bay at Iki Island where the others were killed, the prosecutors announced. A spokesman said the conservationist, Dexter Tate, 36 years old, of Hawaii, was charged with obstructing fishermen's business by force and damaging equipment by cutting nets. There was no explanation for the massing of dolphins around the island. (1974-5)

(Reuters) Sydney, Australia. Little hope given for whales beached in Australia: Members of a pod of false killer whales floundering off Crowdy Beach, 250 miles from Sidney, Australia, as rescue workers look on. Twenty-eight of the sixty mammals that beached themselves Sunday have died, and officials fear the remainder may have to be killed to save a herd of many hundreds that could respond to distress signals from the stranded whales. (June 26, 1985)

I flounder, I beach, I drive myself forward, but the ocean is behind me, not ahead. They think we don't understand this, that we are dumb beasts. The small two-legged upright shapes standing outlined against the light of the sky make noises of worry. They think we are fooled by the echoes of the surf, or lost, or drawn here by some false signal. We have come here on purpose: to die, to lay our bodies in front of your noses, to rot in your sight. *The sea, the sea is dying.* We ride our grief outward to the shore. You do not understand the song we sing, in whispers now, like foam sliding off rock as we lose our voices, this lament, this deathsong.

Can you truly believe we don't know what's happening? Can't feel it? We who chose the ocean, who lived on land long ages ago and returned to the deep home? Do you think we are deaf to the gasping

tearing dying voices of the small fish, have no sense to fear the mons-
trous sponges clinging to those metal tubes of death you hurl down
to us? We can taste death humming in them. We feel the poisons
that filter slowly from the land. We see our kin floating slashed and
hacked along the roads of the sea. We are not weeds gliding past
all this, unknowing. Even the weeds and the tiny plankton know.

Generations of you have hunted us, hunted all our kin, killing us in
greater and greater numbers, sometimes cutting our bodies to pieces
to loose them from your nets when it wasn't even us you meant to
kill. You kill us and don't even use our flesh. We do not understand
why. We only know somehow we must stop you.

You bustle around us anxiously, looking inward, to the deep water,
worried for us. Your concern shows. You fear we will call others, make
a graveyard here before you. You mutter among yourselves wondering how to turn us from this purpose. You think we are crying out
for help. That we are lost, confused, frightened. Yes, we say, but not
lost in these waters, this sand that rubs us raw. Yes, confused, we
do not understand your choices. Frightened. We are very frightened.
Not of the deadly air that dries, that chokes, that kills us. It is not
a tow we need, not help to swim. We are here by choice, riding our
death into your hands. We do not speak your language, but you are
right. These *are* distress signals. It is the world's distress we scream.

I'm On Nature's Side

I'm on nature's side. Man the scientist, *white* man the scientist, white *ruling* class man the scientist, the entrepreneur, the corporation president sets out to control nature—to make it behave!

But I'm a Third World, born working-class woman. I look at it from nature's point of view, from the insects' point of view, the insect out in the cornfield sucking the sweet juice of the crunchy cane or the nourishing mealiness of the newly plumped kernel.

Pest control takes on a different meaning now. Pest control. Why we—you and I—know about pest control right here in this human society. We know all about it.

We know we're pests for wanting to live our lives in peace and plenty. We're pests for not fitting into the grand plan of cornering markets and conquering peoples, increasing profitability and productivity, of sheltering taxes and fixing prices. And we've got to be made to fit in, we've got to be controlled. A la buena o a la mala, or come quietly cause I carry a big stick.

Now those bugs out there in our wheatfields, cornfields, orchards, and gardens, they're out for the same things we are—for a stomach full of grain and a heart full of joy, for love under a green leaf, and sleep under the moon. That makes them pests. To control them, gardeners and agricultural schools, farmers and multinationals spray poisons, distribute infected blankets, unleash predators and armies, demolish nesting sites and villages and neighborhoods. And we die. Many of us die.

But not all. Some of us survive. Our survivors are stronger in some ways, more wily, more versatile. We protect ourselves. We fight back.

We grow in numbers. And they spray more poisons, attack again and again. And we die, and then, we who survive revive and grow in numbers.

And still they maim us and kill us. Still they spray radiation, spray malathion, parathion, agent blue and white and orange, TNT and EDB. No matter how we resist, how often we survive, they spray, because they are so deluded by their power—so sure that when they command, we will obey—that they cannot see what is before them. They cannot even understand that the more they shoot and spray us, the more numerous we become, the more we fight back, the more corn and wheat we eat, until one day we will devastate their crops, bankrupt their agribusiness, destroy their armies, topple their governments.

We will survive!

El Salvador

I know the screen says El Salvador, but surely that's my aunt Josefa pulling the boy away gently. And he's exactly like the boy who lived down the block when I was twelve, sharp boned with deep cocoa eyes in a thin café con leche face. He is as small as he was then but pulling himself tall as his father was before the bullet smacked him to the ground to lie there with his blood spreading slowly in ever widening deltas of red, spreading in pink clouds over the scene and the screen, spreading a jagged crust over his playfulness and gentleness. "Compañeros," he says hoarsely, his spine as straight as a murdering rifle, and somewhere out of sight another woman's voice starts a chant of *"Ay dios, ay dios poderoso."* "Compañeros," he begins again, tears sheeting his face, "mi padre era luchador, combatiente. ¡Esta sangre se vengará!" ("My father was a fighter. His blood will be avenged.") *Ay dios, ay dios poderoso.* "Oh god," I echo, "dear god." Josefa puts her arm around him, turns him away, explains to the camera, to the unseen persons behind the camera, to me, "Muchos compañeros han muerto." and to you, in a soft slow English, "So many people have die." *¡Ay dios todo poderoso!*

Roadkill

It's the daily deaths don't count,
roadkillings.

I walk the country morning road
foot after stepped foot
stop
squat
by the small brown snake its tongue
sensing sensing   its
insides a large sticky tumor by its side.
I see the fly stuck bloody fur, squirrel faced
the thin film of chipmunk color on the tar and stone.

Cars speeding off the lines down the ramps down the road the whole
economy rushing to a higher GNP better profits rising prices on the
stock exchange not noticing not counting not taking to account the
gas the miles the corpses flung in high arcs off the fenders: the dogs
the girls the men the deer. It's the daily deaths don't count.

For Angel, For Vieques

1.

When they came into that hot Florida jail cell, looking up into their faces, did you see your death sentence like a wall across their eyes? Or did the first blow take you by surprise? Did you keep thinking this is just another beating, until suddenly you understood, or your flesh understood for you: they weren't holding any punches, they weren't going to stop? How much of a consolation was it, knowing the exact reason for your death?

2.

The whitest beaches in the world. Water so clear you can see fish move through coral reefs sixty feet down. Low clouds drifting in the sea breeze trail their blue shadows across the translucent waves, and for a moment, darken the green land.

3.

Look again. This is the landscape of war: the whitest beach, the greenest hill, earth pitted and scarred into a family likeness: the familiar, pock-marked face of Viet Nam, showing up here in our family—little sister, Isla Nena. Ships, jets, tanks, trucks, bombs and bombs and bombs. The noise cracks the walls of the houses. Even the sea dawn of the Caribbean is shell-blasted. This is an island the U.S. Navy wanted for target practice.

4.

People live here, crowded into densely packed strips of terrain. The cattle farmers are allowed to graze their animals on the shorn and now eroding hills alongside the impact areas. Here and there a dead cow shows the effects of straying. The cow should have stayed where it belonged, says the Navy. Angel's face, beaten and bruised in that cell. The flies settling on the blood, and no hand brushing them off. You should have stayed where you belonged.

5.

The cattlemen are allowed the use of the hills, but the sea is fenced in with regulations. PRIVATE PROPERTY says the sea these days. NO TRESPASSING. These boats have worked the water for generations. These brown-faced people know every shape of food or danger belonging to salt water. Now they are told, PRIVATE PROPERTY—this ancient hunting of fish, the craft, the weapon, the hunting ground. PRIVATE PROPERTY the waking before dawn to place the nets and traps. PRIVATE PROPERTY, the coming to shore with a good catch. WE OWN THE SEA. WE OWN YOUR LIVES. THE DIFFERENCE IS, WE NEED THE SEA. For target practice.

6.

Operation Springboard, they call it, or Readex. A dress rehearsal for murder. The Chilean Navy pretends it is Valparaiso in 1973. The U.S. Marines imagine it's the Dominican Republic in 1965, Grenada in 1983. It was almost Nicaragua, 1979. It may still be Nicaragua . . . 1984, '85, '86. The perfect imitation invasion. Each year the Navy rents out our destruction at a thousand bucks an hour.

7.

Under a large moon that gives each leaf a knife edge of light, we plant the torn earth. When we leave, an army of seedlings is camped at the crater's edge. In the morning the sign reads: THIS ACRE HAS BEEN RECLAIMED BY THE CRUSADE FOR THE RESCUE OF VIEQUES.

8.

Five a.m. All heat has left this room. The body that was on the floor is hanging from the ceiling. In a few hours, prison officials will discover a "suicide." (The Navy calls in its experts to testify that the song of the tree frogs is actually *louder* than the jets). The prison officials will testify that Angel *could* have beaten himself.

9.

Sea, ancient sea. Wide illuminated sea of our dreaming and waking. Green and blonde land. Cricket bound, bird hidden island of mangrove and naked hill. Between the elusive fire of phosphorescent bay, and the slow, brown downbeat of the pelican's noon flight, under the strands of barbed wire and the warning signs, our life is still the thickest, the toughest root.

10.

Slipping past the signs, we walked through the sleeping camp, that safeguard of U.S. national security, and made our way to the water to place our bodies between the gunner and the target. Offshore, the warships. The bishop held a service, and we all sang. Then: jeep, truck, jeep, soldiers. The guards pull and arrest, shove and club and arrest. The bishop is arrested. An old woman is dragged along the beach and arrested. They are charged with trespassing, which means being on your own land when somebody else wants it. Some of them are sent to federal penitentiaries in the States. One of them is sent to Florida. To that cell.

II.

Angel, your jail cell death is a cold sweat on my skin. It's getting bloodier, closer to home. Vieques, this Viet Nam bomb-blasted landscape is a nightmare at the back of my eyes, a taste there, photographs of a war that all the time gets bloodier and bloodier and closer to home.

Puerto Rico Journal

2/14/83 (on the plane)

Home. I'm going home, I thought, and the happiness bubbled in me and spilled over. Home to the broad split leaves of the plantain and banana, the gawky palm, the feathery tree fern, to the red bell of the hibiscus and the yellow trumpets of the canario, to the warm moist sweet smell of the air. Heavy and light at the same time, heavy with moisture but blowing lightly from the sea. My tongue has been clipped and trimmed and trained, but my heart is all softness, like the air blowing through the palm leaves. My core is red and orange and bright green, and the turquoise of the sea. I am a tropical child. I carry my island tucked inside and I'm going home.

2/16/83

But this was never home! We're staying at Samuel's apartment in the heart of the city, and I bounce around Santurce like a tourist. It's exciting—not knowing the streets, where the bus goes, where to shop, what I'll find. It's a foreign city for me for all I lived eleven years in Puerto Rico. But all of it in the countryside, and I'm more at home with the vegetation than with this city's streets.

Home, like Australians talking about an England they have never seen. The home country: Italy, Ireland, Poland, Puerto Rico. Photographs, someone else's memories and my vivid dreams as I grew up. Home? A place where I am never completely at home. But then where am I completely at home? I spent the day at El Yunque drawing leaves and flowers, the moss-covered trunks of the mountain palm, the thrusting inflorescences of bedraggled-looking bromeliads. These are my closest friends on the island, the flora. And the fauna: lagartijos, and coquís, the tody bird, and the lizard cuckoo.

2/18/83

Living here is science fiction. I've read so many stories that imagine another world existing at the same time and place as this one but in another dimension and then something happens and that other dimension enters yours and strange people appear in the living room and sit in your chairs. At Samuel's, our bedroom is crossed with other parallel lives, and I smell the rich smell of the beans for someone else's supper as if I were cooking it. Habichuelas—puertorican beans not Boston—the stew rich with garlic and onions, oregano, and achiote. Someone's cocks crow right under my pillow startling me awake at 4:00 a.m. and all through the back alleys of this metropolis other cocks answer. The chickens scratch all day and the cock's cries go out on the bean-scented air again and again.

Now it's pork chops. The fried pork smell is heavy and pungent, laced with burnt garlic. I hear a child and I look around bewildered, expecting a hammock or a crib next to my chest of drawers. Someone is angry and slamming doors in the empty air in front of the jalousied windows.

I've slipped inside their lives. I live like a person without skin in a house without walls. I could be them. I am, and there is comfort in that. But mostly I yearn for thick stone walls and heavy wooden doors and shutters. I yearn for the cold, for the closing in and closing off of winter, for layers of clothes, and the deep silence of a northern woods.

2/19/83

A ladder, a careful climb over the roof of the marquesina, a long step onto the flat cement roof, and then you're in another world. This is where the trees go when they leave Calle Isabel. Here are the tops of my father's trees. This is where mangos and mangotínes fall when they ripen. He moves about, picking off dead leaves. Birds hop from branch to branch, from tree to tree. I see the avocado in front of the house at face level. I see flat rooftops peeking out from acres of green branch and leaf.

While my father tidies his trees I sit down and sketch the mango, its weight manifest in its off-center curves, in the plumb line of the stem it drops from. The leaves are long, elegant, dark green, curling, curving, folding like draperies out from their center veins.

My father tells the same stories over and over, the ones I first heard decades ago, stories about work, his mates, his foreman. He gives advice. He talks and talks and doesn't listen. He's never listened. Now, in his old age, he doesn't hear.

This is the one place I can be at peace with him. He tells me how he cares for the trees, how he prunes for yield. He shows me the scars on the thick branches and the new growth. He tells me how greedy his neighbors are for the fruit, how generous he is with it when it ripens.

I listen. Or not. My thoughts mostly on the lines of the leaf, the one just above the straight-as-a-die stem. Its the only way I've found so far to be with him and not wish I were miles away. I want to be here, to say goodbye while he recognizes me, calls me by my own name.

"The birds pull apart our mops for their nests," he says. I've seen those mops, ragged, torn. He doesn't chase the birds away the way he chases people. I smile. No wonder I like the birds, the mango, the alegria, better than the people.

2/23/83

I'm feeling so sad, so depressed. I think it has to do with going up to Indiera Baja. I associate it with death, death of friends, of houses, of a way of life. I wish I could disconnect Indiera from those images.

The need to avoid places—avoid my feelings—makes the landscape dangerous. My mental map is marked with red X's, with land mines of fear and sadness. I don't want to see our houses or Jane's grave, to see the disintegration. I feel helpless, a familiar feeling. I can't stop the damage to important things, and I think of my father throwing away my childhood papers when I moved out. I still mourn them.

2/24/83

This is not home. Eleven years couldn't make it home. I'll always be clumsy with the language, always resentful of the efforts to re-make me, to do what my parents couldn't manage. What? What is it they couldn't manage? I don't know for sure, but it has to do with the kind of woman I am. Nothing so crude as docile, catholic woman-hood...Lots of women here are strong and independent. And yet...

I don't know. Maybe it has to do with not having been a little girl in this place. I was shaped on Manhattan Island.

I remember in the mountains how women said "Mi marido no me deja," my husband won't let me. And when someone nagged at me and wouldn't take no for an answer, I'd say it too. It was unanswerable, everyone understood that: "Él no me deja." ¡Pero tu lo dejas que no te deje!

Ironic. On the plane down I'm conscious only of my soft tropical core. Here I'm only aware of the North American scaffolding sur-rounding it, holding it up.

2/27/83

Aurora comes here and says, yes, this is still home. I come here and say this is too much like home for comfort, too many people nag-ging, harping, pushing you into line, into feminine behavior, into

caution and fear, provocativeness and manipulativeness, full of preda-
tory males who punish you for being female. Little freedom of thought
and action, freedom to expand, grow, dare to do something different, to change. Not for my parents' daughter.

I experience Puerto Ricans in Puerto Rico the way I experienced
my home growing up, the way sheep must experience sheepdogs,
the pressure on my flanks, pushing, pushing, the nip at my heels
when I move off on my own. I've been longing for Cambridge for
my bed my room my cloth my wool my pictures my friends. The U.S.
is home now. None of this is home.

Only the lagartijos and the mango trees, the wet growth of El Yunque, the shrill cries of the hawks in the sky, and the housetop forests
around my parents' house. Right now, right here—only the landscape
is home.

2/27/83 (Hacienda Juanita)

Yesterday on the way up from Sábana Grande I thought, I don't want
to be here. I didn't. The roads feel dusty and unappetising, the country
hostile to me, the social life enredada and constricting, and I want
to escape to Cambridge.

I'm afraid of feeling strange in my old home, of feeling bereft. I feel
it now, and I'm writing more to find a way around it than to give
it expression. I am sad that I cannot go back to it. I was happiest
there, in Jane and César's house, after her death. I wasn't haunted
by her, her presence was benign. What has changed?

I am making something awful of the cracking and destruction of
the grave markers I made for my friends. Maga's is all to pieces. Dick
found me one small fragment. I'll take it with me. All Jane's says
is, "Jane Speed de Andreu," in my printing.

2/27/83 (En Indiera Baja)

It was strange seeing the glacis full of rusting cars, the familiar kitchen with someone else's pots. Word of our visit had scurried up the mountain and Ginín was ready for us. She was shelling the just-picked pods for an arroz con gandules. She greeted me as a friend even though we were never neighbors when I lived here. Hers is the kindness of the countryside, especially of the women, that I have always relied on.

The old house down the hill, the one we lived in when we first came here thirty-two years ago, is only a wall or two, some floor joists, a few floor boards, nothing more. I balance on the beam of what was once my bedroom and look south toward the coast and see the Canibal house on the hill opposite, the hills hiding San Germán, the small indentation in the coastline that is Guánica, and the sea— the view that was once my daily companion. That time has long been gone. Now I know it.

2/28/83 (Castañer)

The trip alone would have been worth it, a car's width of road taped to the blade of the ridge, the plunging cliffs on both sides of it and sharp green hills rising and falling about us like storm waves. And then, there it was, Lencho and Gina's house perched on the road's edge, with their farm slanting down from it thick with bananas, malangas, oranges, coffee, flowers—and Gina standing among them with a machete growing out of her hand.

She hugged us and fed us—yes, arroz con gandules—and their own cabbage in a slaw. I laughed with Lencho. He'd sent me a picture of himself with a glass of make-believe rum in his hand as a joke. We're both of us sober now. I toured the house noticing each convenience. Their prosperity calmed me, released my fear for them, for us all.

3/1/83

I went to El Yunque to lay my ghosts. I gathered the stiff waxy leaves, mottled red and green, that lie in the litter, the blossoms of the alegria, red and salmon pink, the small hairy kernels de la palma de la sierra. I had the pool area and the misty rain to myself and as I went round the pool I said my name, their names—Sari, Jane, César, Maga, Josefa, Gregorio, María. All my dead but one died here, on this island, and as I've traveled around it I've carried them in a heart sagging with the weight of it. Maga, Gregorio, Josefa, María, my young self, César, Jane—go! Rest. Be at peace.

The palm seeds make small plops in the water. I will remember you. Red petals float. Stay here in the cool shadows. The leaves join their cousins in flat mats of tan and bright color. Go.

3/2/83

Back at Samuel's apartment. Even the mangos seem to fall inside the room after slithering through the branches. Rustlerustlewhishthud, a mango falls on my bedroom floor. Leafleafleafbranchleafthud—another. Morning chatter of birds in the room, bananaquits, grassquits. They perch and dart through chatter on the dresser, by the lamp, leave, return, leave.

It has been a hard, wearying trip. I look forward to my own life as to a rest cure. I've been anticipating the return home so much, and now as I pack for it, I'm sad about leaving. Ah me, no peace.

Puerto Rico isn't a place I come to be peaceful. Parents, numerous relatives, and too many ghosts. A place of real dependency for me, with Dick a necessary adjunct for safety so much of the time. I pass the place where Pat got chased by men. I feel like the Black woman in Olivia Butler's *Kindred,* sucked into the past, the South, the slave condition.

3/3/83

The atmosphere on this plane is completely changed since the passengers got off at Philadelphia. Before, we'd sat cramped in our cubbies. Now the plane empties out leaving only tanned New Englanders and leg room. We spread out, stand, stretch, joke, talk. We comment on the temperature, the empty seats, the new passengers. Bare toed or shod, sitting up or lying across three seats, we're pals. I'm stretched out with my journal on my lap. I have to smile. I've written, "I'm going home."

Puertoricanness

It was Puerto Rico waking up inside her. Puerto Rico waking her up at 6:00 a.m., remembering the rooster that used to crow over on 59th Street and the neighbors all cursed "that damn rooster," but she loved him, waited to hear his harsh voice carving up the Oakland sky and eating it like chopped corn, so obliviously sure of himself, crowing all alone with miles of houses around him. She was like that rooster.

Often she could hear them in her dreams. Not the lone rooster of 59th Street (or some street nearby. . . she had never found the exact yard though she had tried), but the wild careening hysterical roosters of 3:00 a.m. in Bartolo, screaming at the night and screaming again at the day.

It was Puerto Rico waking up inside her, uncurling and shoving open the door she had kept neatly shut for years and years. Maybe since the first time she was an immigrant, when she refused to speak Spanish in nursery school. Certainly since the last time, when at thirteen she found herself between languages, between countries, with no land feeling at all solid under her feet. The mulberry trees of Chicago, that first summer, had looked so utterly pitiful beside her memory of flamboyan and banana and. . . . No, not even the individual trees and bushes but the mass of them, the overwhelming profusion of green life that was the home of her comfort and nest of her dreams.

The door was opening. She could no longer keep her accent under lock and key. It seeped out, masquerading as dyslexia, stuttering, halting, unable to speak the word which will surely come out in the wrong language, wearing the wrong clothes. Doesn't that girl know how to dress? Doesn't she know how to date, what to say to a professor, how to behave at a dinner table laid with silver and crystal and too many forks?

Yesterday she answered her husband's request that she listen to the whole of his thoughts before commenting by screaming, "This is how we talk. I will not wait sedately for you to finish. Interrupt me back!" She drank pineapple juice three or four times a day. Not Lotus, just Co-op brand, but it was piña, and it was sweet and yellow. And she was letting the clock slip away from her into a world of morning and afternoon and night, instead of "five-forty-one-and-twenty seconds —beep."

There were things she noticed about herself, the Puertoricanness of which she had kept hidden all these years, but which had persisted as habits, as idiosyncracies of her nature. The way she left a pot of food on the stove all day, eating out of it whenever hunger struck her, liking to have something ready. The way she had lacked food to offer Elena in the old days and had stamped on the desire to do so because it *was* Puerto Rican: *Come, mija. . .¿quieres café?* The way she was embarrassed and irritated by Ana's unannounced visits, just dropping by, keeping the country habits after a generation of city life. So unlike the cluttered datebooks of all her friends, making appointments to speak to each other on the phone days in advance. Now she yearned for that clocklessness, for the perpetual food pots of her childhood. Even in the poorest houses a plate of white rice and brown beans with calabaza or green bananas and oil.

She had told Sally that Puerto Ricans lived as if they were all in a small town still, a small town of six million spread out over tens of thousands of square miles, and that the small town that was her country needed to include Manila Avenue in Oakland now, because she was moving back into it. She would not fight the waking early anymore, or the eating all day, or the desire to let time slip between her fingers and allow her work to shape it. Work, eating, sleep, lovemaking, play—to let them shape the day instead of letting the day shape them. Since she could not right now, in the endless bartering of a woman with two countries, bring herself to trade in one-half of her heart for the other, exchange this loneliness for another perhaps harsher one, she would live as a Puerto Rican lives en la isla, right here in north Oakland, plant the bananales and cafetales of her heart around her bedroom door, sleep under the shadow of their bloom and the carving hoarseness of the roosters, wake to blue-rimmed white enamel cups of jugo de piña and plates of guineo verde, and heat pots of rice with bits of meat in them on the stove all day.

There was a woman in her who had never had the chance to move through this house the way she wanted to, a woman raised to be like those women of her childhood, hardworking and humorous and clear. That woman was yawning up out of sleep and into this cluttered daily routine of a Northern California writer living at the edges of Berkeley. She was taking over, putting doilies on the word processor, not bothering to make appointments, talking to the neighbors, riding miles on the bus to buy bacalao, making her presence felt . . . and she was all Puerto Rican, every bit of her.

Nostalgia

Nostalgia for Puerto Rico. I grew up with it, felt it even before I first visited there the summer I turned ten. I have a picture of me sitting on a boat with my uncle Sergio, pert in a new dress with a swinging skirt and a head covered with long sausage curls. I remember visiting my father's family farm, the Morales place in El Hoyo—the hole—a deep valley in the northeastern hills of Puerto Rico. Going swimming with cousins and uncles and aunts in a deep pool in the river. The girls bathed in their slips, and the skirts of the cotton garments billowed about our shoulders in the water as we jumped in again and again. I remember visiting Carmelita on the edge of town—Naranjito. She lived in the old Morales house with the long flight of cement steps up to the high board house, brown and green and white—green with moss and plants and brown with old wood. The magic of playing with my cousin in the dense growth behind her house. She had built a playhouse out of branches and banana leaves and she had a fire laid out between stones and we went to the back door to beg some food from her mother. I can still see it from a ten-year old's height, the door above me and tía Carmelita in it giving us real café con leche to heat on the real fire between the real stones on the real little house in the high jungles of tropical growth that towered green and fragrant above our heads.

I grew up in the chasms of New York City streets, shuttling between a sixth-story apartment and school, the apartment and the park, the apartment and the church. I grew up on my father's stories of sliding down wet hillsides on a banana leaf, green slippery sleds; of climbing orange trees and sitting on a fat branch peeling the fruit carefully con su cortapluma, cutting off a cap to suck the crisp juice, the puertorican way of eating oranges—sucking them dry.

I grew up with nostalgia for a place I did not grow up in, nostalgia for the family I'd missed, uncles and aunts and cousins—and grandparents: Abuela Mercedes, Abuelo Lolo, Abuela Rosario. I grew up with nostalgia for green landscapes and tropical fruit, for broad leaves and red flowers, for the smell of coffee roasting, the sound of cocks crowing and hens scratching behind the house. I grew up wanting blue skies and rain falling in hard punishing drops. I grew up yearning for trees, yearning for trees.

Old Countries

New York is the Old Country to me. Childhood memories of the four years that I lived there, between the squirrels and stone walls of Riverside Park, and the thrilling roar, the musty winds, and glittering sidewalks of the subway, are laid, thin as silverplate on an old spoon, over an iron core of older memories. The garment district and my grandmother's hands at the sewing machine, stitching up bras and girdles with the other Puerto Rican women; my mother's fable about the essence of the city—a man she once saw leading a goat into the subway; my step-grandpa Abe's sister who died in the Triangle Shirtwaist fire; my great-grandma Leah and her husband Abe and her sister Betty, all working in the garment trade during the years of unionization; my aunt Eva the hatmaker and her radical Finnish husband Einar. They were the people who lived in my Old Country, who had lived there in the days of the big strikes. In the days of the big hunger called The Depression.

The names of streets and neighborhoods, spoken casually by native New Yorkers, are full of meaning to me, with bits of history clinging to them like earth to a shoe: Amsterdam Avenue and Harlem, a ferment of Black culture, politics, movement; Brownsville where my father was born among the other immigrants, and Coney Island home of Nathan's hotdogs and the big parachute ride; Bridgeport, where Pop worked in a factory and slept in a rooming house five nights a week, eating his meals at Chopick's; the Lower East Side, home of both my peoples, mysterious with smells and faces and eateries and the trailing threads of friends and cousins and neighbors last heard of in 1934 or '47 or '59.

I grew up in a rainforest, hearing, like earlier immigrant children, of the horrors and delights of the Old Country. Schools there were called PS and then a number. There were neighborhoods with lines as clearly marked as any international border: Italian, Irish, Polish, Black, Jewish, Chinese, and the new populations seeping in: Puerto Ricans, Dominicans, Haitians, Jamaicans, Cubans. In the old country they sold hot chestnuts on the street ("What's a chestnut, mami?" I think, sucking on a fresh-picked orange), and there were vendors who sold hot yams. My mother bought one every day she could and held it to keep her hands warm.

I heard that my father lived in his street the way I did on my hillside, knowing the neighbors and what they did when they grew up, each neighborhood a little homeland. That my mother loved kosher pickles and learned to knit from immigrant Eastern European Jews. How she watched her friend Moira smear forbidden lipstick on her mouth by the light of a street lamp, in the mirror of a glass door. How the Puerto Ricans called the police "la jara" after O'Hara, because so many of them were Irish. How the Irish kids beat up and insulted and threw stones at the Jews, my mother among them. How my father was beaten up by anti-Semites and learned how to fight.

I am earth and bone from the green mountains of Indiera. As my grandparents were from the hills of Naranjito. As my great grandparents were from the forests and farmlands of Yaza, where my great-grandfather Abraham Sakhnin heard from his father stories of an older Lithuanian home, left five generations before in the days of Tsar Nicholas I (ancestor, as Pop would say, of Tsar Nicholas the last).

I am a mountain-born, country-bred, homegrown jíbara child. But I have inherited all the cities through which my people passed, and their dust has sifted and settled onto the black soil of my heart. Kirovograd, the forbidden gentile streets where Pop bribed his way into a job. Granada of the Moors, where the great Mosque rises. Barcelona on the sea. Jerusalem the Holy, and Cairo, and Damascus. Bustling Ife, and Luanda, and Dakar. *Mine are great ports of the immigrants:* Odessa, Liverpool, Bristol, Lisboa, Marseille, Cadiz, Amsterdam, Abidjan, Accra, Lagos. *The places of arrival are mine:* New Orleans, Montreal, Buenos Aires, Halifax, San Juan, Angel Island, San Francisco, Ellis Island, New York. They were no goldeneh medinas, no gold mountains, no lands of milk and honey, but in those crowded worlds of smoke and soot and hardship, of hunger and illness and ten-hour days, love sent its sturdy roots into the brick. A dozen languages rang out in song and argument between the tenement walls, bringing those dingy streets alive.

Even Chicago, grim old gritty dust heap of a city, had its blues its trains, had its Northern Black Irish Polish Russian Hillbilly Puerto Rican Ojibwe meatpacking railroad citylake city spirit, worthy of love.

I didn't yearn for the cities the way my mother did for greenness and quiet and trees. But I dreamt of them. The smell and confusion of them. The streets full of people. The alleys and avenues. The markets and neighborhoods. The stories hidden in their names, and the ingenuity of the people who made it home. The bustling variety of life, of languages, of foods, of customs—the meeting of so many roads.

City Pigeons

Bird!
You are of the same breed as me,
shitting on the same statues:
                    dead politicians
                    dead generals
                    dead gods
dipping down to the same gutter stream
same curbstone, stoopstep, streetside
feeding on the same crumbs
running from the same bums
                    boys
                    cops
                    noise
flying from the same stench
                    car puke
                    bus belch
up on the same ledges
out on the same limbs—
                    fountain rims
flying up on the same currents
taking off from the same premises
to the same sky's-the-limit if the planes don't fly too low
and, oh honey, the planes do fly too low.

Oh, we are of the same breed, you and I
off the same park bench, off the same damned tree.
City birds of a common feather, you and me.

Beneath The Skin Where The Light Comes From

Destitution

I was born in August 1930. I have always feared destitution, always. Even before I was born, the fear seeped in with my nutriments through the thin capillary walls of my placenta into my heart.

My mother was a girl, nineteen, married young because the family store had folded. The older girls all found husbands in a hurry. The older boy lowered his sights, became a policeman instead of a social worker. My mother, shipped to the United States within hours of the marriage ceremony, landed in New York in time for the crash, arrived to recurrent joblessness, discrimination, poverty, fear. I was conceived within months of her arrival.

I could live in luxury: yachts and champagne, diamonds up to my eyebrows, and I would worry about food, about a roof over my head, about whether the money would run out. The Depression is part of every cell of my body. My mother drank it in in her teen years in Naranjito, those years of increasing poverty in the colonies before the stock market crash. My father migrated to New York, escaped long before he married, leaving the pan for the fire. Their anxiety was the breath of life to me, their hunger flavored my milk.

I don't have many stories. The subject was too painful, too frightening, too omen-ous. My mother often slipped quickly over the events, hinting. The stories were told differently every time, like traditional folk tales inherited with the silver rosary. My father never spoke of it at all.

One story: Paco Lopez knew of a job. He told my father about it because in their circle of unemployed he had the greatest need—a wife, a new baby. But it was all the way downtown, and Papi had only one nickel to spare for the subway. So he rode there, got the job, and walked the miles back.

Another: my father wearing my mother's underwear. His had worn out, worn through. She tells me in whispers. "Manolin musn't know I told you." I don't know why.

And the one about me. My mother working in a hospital laundry, leaving her baby to be watched by a woman who cared very little. Mami's eyebrows rise. I imagine unwholesome food, unkindness.

When my teeth stopped developing holes regularly like well-made lace, sometime in my early fifties, I knew I'd caught up with my pregnancies—leaching my teeth and leaving them vulnerable—and with my childhood years: rice and weak coffee instead of vegetables and oranges and milk. I spent my adolescence in dental offices. And when I, too, was poor and pregnant, I pushed dried milk and the vitamins my father sent me into my protesting body, seeing the little girl baby of twenty-five years before in the strange woman's arms.

When I was young I always knew when my parents were out of money. I would sense it like the angle of the sun as winter approaches. I wanted to store nuts in the ground the way my father stores crackers and cereal, rice and cans, cupboards full, fridge full, underwear packed tight in drawers.

So today, when I listened to a woman on television tell about how she survived for months, in winter, in Chicago, living in a car with her two daughters, I listened. I noted how she washed her hair in cold water in public washrooms, how they saved the few nickels and dimes they could garner to wash their clothes regularly, how they slept two in the front seat, the older girl alone in the back because only she had a job as a waitress. I noticed that they managed, that they were clean, that they survived, and I breathed a sigh of relief.

So I asked Dick and he said if it came to that, he would be willing. He promised to wash his feet, in cold water if need be, in public washrooms. If he does that, I know I can handle the rest.

Dairy Queen

Sitting down at the table you can see the thin slice of moon and the evening star in the same pane of the window, out there beyond the pomarosa tree which makes a darker mass in the darkness. It's pitch black, smotheringly dark out there except for the rectangle of yellow light from the window lightening up the bare clay yard, and for those two bright beautiful shapes in the sky. I sit here tonight staring at the western sky at my right, as I do every other night for hours while the star sets, the moon sets, while I wait for Dick to come home.

The house sits all around me, a shell, protecting me from the cold, the night, humanity. Out there is Indiera Baja and among the coffee trees and banana plants, the pomarosas, llagrumos, flamboyanes, and aguacates are little animals prowling, and people—men mostly— coming home drunk from don Paco's or Gloria's store. I can't hear them or see them, I imagine them. They've never hurt me, the men or the animals, but I'm afraid of them.

The house smells of home: of the wooden planks it's made of, of the sawdust from the kitchen we're building, of Lori's fresh-washed diapers sitting folded on the couch, of the boiled roots and eggs she and I had for supper, and of the dark wet plant life outside— fresh, cool, rich—a smell of growth and fermentation, a tropical smell, an earth smell. It comforts me.

The coquís are loud. Their chirping makes a din that echoes in my head like a faraway tide, except for the one that sits under the dish drainer. Its piercing "quí quí quí coquí" startles me. I smile. Lovely little creature.

The grain of the wood in the table top attracts my finger. I run it back and forth, back and forth, along the groove of an old injury. I should sand this, I think, sand it, and repaint it.

I feel the baby kick and push. Quickly I look down and catch the heavy motion under my skin—waves. Alive! It's still alive. I've been so scared. Scared about how thin I've been. Scared to sit here without Dick. Scared when I thought Dick would go to the States to study, leaving me here alone with two babies. Scared now about where we'll end up, what city, what housing, what money. Scared I'd lose this child. I almost lost it; I bled and bled and then lay on my bed, feet raised, for weeks. I'm scared when I pick Lori up or mop the floor. And I'm scared of spending the night alone.

Dick should be home soon. I strain to listen for the sound of the truck. Faintly a small thin sound reaches my ear, all that's left of don Paco's jukebox music after it travels across the hill to me. He's open late tonight. A jeep roars near, past. The clock ticks loudly. It's almost midnight.

There. That's him, still far off but loud. That engine growls, you can hear it for miles. I stand, go to the door. When I open it and let the dark in, it has a friendly face. I can just see my garden huddled down for the night, and the smooth-edged leaves of the avocado tree, can hear the hens shifting, a few gentle clucks.

The truck lights cut through the dark and blind me. He shuts them off. I wait again. He must be getting his things. The metal door squeals open, slams.

"Dick!" "Sari!" I kiss his cheek, his mouth, briefly, take the package from his hands. Dairy Queen!

"¿Vainilla o chocolate?"

"Vainilla. No tenian chocolate hoy. Algo con la máquina..."

"Damn! I wanted chocolate tonight. How was your trip?"

"O.K. It was good coming into the mountains. It was real hot in town today. The breezes were cool at el dieciocho. Wonderful."

Dick's been putting his papers down on the table—a large book, a spiral notebook, a folder. I've been reaching for the bowls, the spoons. I take the cardboard container out of the paper bag, slip the cover off, carry it in one hand, the bowls and spoons in the other, my large abdomen between them keeping them separate.

Dick moves his papers off onto the counter. I start serving the soft cold yellowy whiteness.

"Remember when there was no Dairy Queen?"

"And no milk. . .when all we had was canned evaporated milk."

"Hmm, what a treat. So did you look at stars today?"

Under his mustache his mouth is full of Dairy Queen. He looks tired. Bags under his eyes. A sagging to his cheeks. Too tired, too old looking for twenty-five. While he tells me about the young man who appeared with one of his students, chaperoning her for the astronomy class because he didn't want his sweetheart out at night "alone" with other men, I look at him and feel sad and sorry. He left at dawn and came back at midnight, for me, because I'm frightened at night, won't sleep those three nights a week without his large comforting body by my side. "Con pena, lo quiero con pena," my mother would say. I love him with pity. I feel like crying.

He falls silent. Eats large bites with pleasure. I slip my spoon into the melted pool and catch the edge of the icy mound. A little bite, a sip, making it last. I want to tell him about today, about Lori, about Pablo, but feel too tired and sad. A bit weak, too, from the end of my terror. Above the coquís and the clock and the thread of a crooned ballad I hear the spoons against the bowl, the wet sounds of our tongues, of our mouths, of Dairy Queen.

A Story

He said this was something that happened in his own city, before he fled for the border with his young wife, who was pregnant. His face is round, childish, shy. His eyes are dark and still. He speaks in a low, even voice as if he could make the words he says lie down, be less sharp, but he can't, and we see that they hurt his throat as they come out and that they hurt his chest when he tried to keep them in.

He says he was walking down a street in his city with a friend. It was dawn, and they were on their way to work. The woman was lying on the pavement, dead. She had been shot in the head. The soldiers had come for her husband, but he was away in the mountains so they killed her instead. He says that she was very pregnant. That she must have been just about due. Her belly was huge. As he passed the body, he saw the child was still alive inside her cooling flesh, moving, pushing, pulsating in her womb. His hands ached to reach into her and pull it free, but the soldiers were still standing at the end of the street, and he knew how quickly and easily they would shoot him, too, if he tried to help. We had to keep walking, he tells me. He has never forgotten the light that beat from that unborn child, trapped in its dead mother's body. He said it filled the street with a flickering radiance, like the sun reflected in water, that it peeled the paint from the walls, bleached the wood, and left strange, pale marks on his skin for days.

Birth

1.

I lay in a bed in the small bedroom hurting horribly. I hurt as if I were giving birth, a sharp pain piercing front to back through my uterus, a labor pain continuous and unlooked for. Only three months pregnant and I was bleeding. I knew I was losing the child.

Where was everybody? This house was always so full of people arguing, making noise, minding my business, and now when I needed someone, anyone, to hold my hand, to hold me, there was no one at all.

I wish I were in my own home, not here with his family. Or at least with my mother who would touch me, who would know how sad I was, how my chest hurt from the iron ache of loss.

2.

I sat in the cemetery of a bathroom and pushed it out with the last of my cramps. I stood there and looked at the blood-stained waters pink against the chill white of the porcelain toilet bowl. And with my heart like a great lead plumb bob hanging on a string from my mouth, I looked down, stared down, at a beautiful soft grey saucer frilled like a sunbonnet, floating like a dead jellyfish, my baby only a small red blob off center, my hopes as dead as my child, and oh how I want to go back and stop standing there storing up the sight of it for a lifetime. Oh, I want to reach out, reach in and hold it, cup it in the palm of my hand. It was my creation, a wonder—my child, my own, my sweet.

3.

"What does she need another baby for? What's the hurry? Dick has enough to worry him. Why did he have to go and marry so young. A Puerto Rican, no less! Right away she starts having children. Sometimes I think she's still a Catholic. She called me into the bathroom— to look at it—like it was something to look at. She wanted to keep it to show the doctor. I ask you, what's to show? I flushed it down. I hope she has the sense to wait now."

4.

I could serve a platter of placenta
Young, quite fresh and delicately braised
Garnished with parsley
Set it in front of the cold hard faces
that mock and sneer at the near mother's pain
and towering large and menacing
Invite: *Ess, ess mein kind.*
Eat!

5.

Where do the sewers of Manhattan Beach go, and what fish feed on miscarried pregnancies? Dear creature, I watched you move slowly through the swirling waters and down the toilet, down under the brick and stucco houses of Manhattan Beach, under Sheepshead Bay with its bright white yachts and work-soiled fishing boats and out, out to sea, out of reach, out of sight. I never said goodbye. Goodbye. Goodbye! May the fish have nibbled gently at your sweet grey frills.

The Grandmother Time

And now my ovaries have laid down their task
and are resting, grazing, in fallopian pastures.

*"¿Cúando viene la cría?" the woman would ask touching my belly.
"¿Y cuando viene la cría?" When will my children come? Months of
hoarding stored sperm in my cupped vagina, sitting on the privy
seat bent over my arms, crying, my blood on my hand.*

I wanted babies, always wanted them, ached for them, reached for
them, each of them, every single one I saw. My eyes still turn to them,
years of habit dying hard. I admire them, still crave the swansdown
of their skin, the curves of their fat bellies and buttocks, their tight
little calves, the round fragility and hardness of their skulls, the grip
of their tiny fingers, the clever mobility of their feet and toes.

I still look. I sometimes touch. But when my friend put her first-
born in my arms, my breath stopped. I did all the right things when
he cried but as soon as she left the room, I gave him to Dick and
went into the kitchen to breathe.

*Sweet and pungent child served
on a bed of tired toys, garnished
with blanket à la baby pee, topped
with sour milk sauce, redolent
of society, redolent
of deep sleep*

I can no longer bear to be around the very young for very long. I get ailments, get headaches, indigest my food, lose sleep. I feel dulled and flattened as if I had pressed in, pressed down to keep my misered feelings from escaping, to keep from yelling aiii mami, aiii mami, the way I screamed as I gave birth—the nurses clucking with disapproval—aaaii mami, help me, I'm in pain.

(from my journal, November 1954) *Up at dawn. Aurora heard the rooster crow and the dogs bark at Dick with his load of cabbage for the hospital. She is now in her crib, crying one minute, smiling the next. But what smiles. Nose crinkling, lip stretching, cheek puffing smiles. Time to give her the breast. I love to feed her and hold her warm, round body close. I love to watch her asleep, to smell her spicy sweaty odor.*

I dream about them tiny, small enough to fit in the palm of my hand, miniature dolls, with skulls of paper-thin celluloid, skulls I could dent with a careless finger. I dream afraid. I don't dream of their warm roundness, their goatlike smell, the love I felt like a pain, the tickling and giggling and gurgling, the learning as natural as breath. I don't dream of the pleasure.

Saturated
Saturated
with their wails
their wants
their touch me!
hold me!
feed me!
with look, mami!
when will we get there?
she hit me first!
give me one!
I'm scared.
I hurt me!
you hurt me!
the crying crying crying
the noise of it
the pain
piercing my ears
my skull
knifing my lungs till I fill
full
with cries
with want
my want
with give me
give me now
till SPLAT
I burst!
bits of skin and longing splattering
the just-washed floor
the children's hands
their eyes, sucked
into their open mouths
like air.

A limb gone numb. I dare not let it come alive. I think I believe that if I remember all the joy, all the love, I will drown in the thin air I breathed all those years, my nostrils barely above the rising waters, almost drowning in all of it, the care, the self-denial, the endless tasks, *more than I can do! more than I can do!* How could I keep them safe? I know now I didn't. How could I give them enough when I felt I had so little. And how, now, can I be trusted around these new ones when I have learned to see the weaknesses clear through me, great jagged cracks that could open wide to consume your babies, that could swallow up their tender bodies. How?

But these are not my children. Other people will wake in the night now, will go through their days leaden with exhaustion, weighted with care. Others will stand guard over that small being's fragility.

I force my eyes to my new, my grandparental task, narrow as the strips of cloth I cut for the welcoming quilt, the scissors slicing with a gritting sound, enjoying their meal. I lay out the pieces on the floor, the candy stripes sliding smoothly through my fingers, red pink, rose pink, night blue, the colors vibrating in each other's company. Now I will sew.

Aurora's Jewish great-grandparents on Brooklyn's Brighton Beach boardwalk (1965). Abraham Sakhnin came from the Ukraine to the United States in 1904. His wife Leah followed two years later with their daughter Ruth and other family members.

Aurora's grandmother Ruth Sackman (changed from the original *Sakhnin* by immigration officials on Ellis Island), at age fourteen (1918), wearing "my first fancy dress."

Rosario reading to Aurora at home in Maricao, Puerto Rico.

Aurora's second birthday (1956), a portrait of Lenin and a Puerto Rican flag on the wall. The flag was made in the 1940s by Mary Craik Speed (Maga), Jane Speed's mother, and displayed at a time when doing so could lead to arrest.

Dick Levins, Aurora's father, teaching her to write.

Rosario, age twelve (on the left), with her father Manuel Morales, her mother Aurora (Lola), and her sister Gloria.

My
Roots
Are
Not
My
Own
Alone

Of Course She Read

Of course my daughter read when she was little, of course she spoke so well so soon. She spoke for me. She said what I never dared. She said "I won't," she said "I want," she said "You're a bad mami," she said "Give me that," she said "I will!"

Of course she read when she was little. She was my first-born. And while I nursed her I had a book in my free hand. I had all of Jane's books and Maga's books and César's books to consume. I had Dick's family Dickens to work my way through. As her tiny rooting mouth sucked my milk, I sucked something from those books I was born wanting.

Of course she read when she was little. She was born hungry, born small, crying for food, feeding continuously, so that I never slept. I cried with tiredness and shook the cradle with despair. I won't feed you, I cried, I won't, I won't. But I did.

Of course she read when she was little. I was hungry for words when she was born. My mother was poor, went hungry when I was born, but I was hungry for stories, for books. I was trying to catch up, trying to make up for starting at thirteen. Too old for *Alice*, too old for *Wind in the Willows*, too old by a hair for *Little Women*, but I read them, read more, read faster, to catch up because no one read me picture books when I was two and my father gave me one when I was twelve. Too old. Too old. Someday I will have caught up, I prayed, someday I will have read enough soon enough.

Of course she read when she was little. I'd had only one shelf of books when I was growing up—the big Spanish dictionary and the *Hamlet* my father found on the high school steps, the *Reader's Digest*s and the picture book. Someday, I thought, I will have books, a hundred books, a thousand books.

Of course she read when she was little. I'd said, I will have a child and read him picture books, read her story books, read them to them over and over. Someday I will have books on high shelves so little grubby hands won't crayon the pages. I will have books on low shelves for them to reach and read, to touch and know. I will read *Alice* and *Wind in the Willows* and *Little Women*. I will read Dickens and *Winnie the Pooh* and *Charlotte's Web*.

And I did.

Synagogue

1.

I was scared when I'd done it, crossed myself in the name of the Father and the Son and the Holy Ghost in front of the Synagogue that I passed almost every day on the way to school, to the supermarket, the subway. I moved my hand automatically in the ritual pattern: forehead-chest-shoulder-shoulder, a gesture I used crossing in front of altars, in front of churches and that I still use to ward off unpleasant fates, the way others knock wood. I'd do it and look around to see if anyone had noticed, afraid someone would slip out of the tall imposing door cut into the corner of the dark brick building and see me. No one ever did.

I'd do it without thought, as I hurried past on my way somewhere else, my subconscious recognizing the building as a kind of church, like my beloved St. Athanasius a block away. But what would the bearded man with the yarmulke floating on top of his hair think, the man I imagined coming out of the door? That I was fending off Jewishness?

I was afraid he would. I'd learnt enough about what was happening to the Jews in Europe since I'd moved out of El Barrio where I'd gone to grade school, where I knew only one Jewish girl. Her father owned the butcher shop on the same block as the school, and I asked her why the Jews killed Christ. I remembered that with painful shame six years later in the 1940s every time I crossed myself in front of the Synagogue unthinkingly. I knew now who it was did the killing, who did the dying.

2. Tiffany Street

After thirteen I grew up Jewish. Well, *one* of my worlds was Jewish, 100 percent Jewish, except for me. No, including me, because that was my place to become Jewish. I asked Lorna to teach me Yiddish, and I can still write *tish* for table—*tish, tishel, tishele*—a little table, the littlest table holding only those few letters and the one song, so that I sit like all the other young ones born in this country—the amerikaner—sit smiling a silly uncomprehending smile at the joke in Yiddish while the others shout their laughter so that she turns to us and starts the story over again in English. "A Jew and a Gentile went to heaven. . ."

Old Mrs. Abrams was orthodox, kept the dietary laws, kept kosher, kept all the holidays but her children broke the fast on Yom Kippur, ate bacon, made fun of her on the streets. "Tref! Tref!" her daughter shouted, like old Mrs. Abrams. "Mumble, mumble," she mimicked, muttering words to make it kosher, pretending to swing a dead chicken over her head to make their transgressions clean, so that I almost saw it, the pale stubble of the pin feathers pricking its bumpy skin, naked and cold and ridiculous in the Bronx air over her head.

We'd stand in front of the mailboxes in the entryway to her house, Moira and I, while she put her lipstick on. I wouldn't, and wouldn't stuff a bra with cotton under a tight sweater, wouldn't kiss the boys or my friends' fathers. I looked on, the good girl, the "good influence," the anchor her mother hoped would slow her down. We'd stand in front of the mirror and check the space between our thighs, the one that had to disappear if we were ever to become women. Or sit on my bed and talk God, question his existence, question our questioning, clarifying the broth, decanting the wine of our belief, throwing the sludge away with our used sanitary napkins.

Spineless, Lorna taunted. She wanted me to stand up to her, stand up for myself, stand up to my religion, give up god for lent. But who would Watson her Sherlock, play the victim to her Nazi spy, if not I? Besides, my father was a much more single-minded tyrant than she, and he would beat my bones to powder if I stood too straight and looked him in the eye. She despaired of me, so stiff with the boys. Relax and enjoy it! But all Harry got when he grabbed were my clenched teeth. With every tight muscle I fought off that kiss like rape, and fought off a rape like that kiss, never too sure of the difference. Lorna led to me the A's in the library, passing on her ambition to read the whole building through, like breaking her last candy bar in two, sharing it with me. Oh Lorna, I taste it still.

I wouldn't smile either. Mrs. Rabinowicz lived in a few small rooms with a silent husband, a disillusioned son, and a wandering daughter, her face closed to what she'd left behind in Germany, to the big apartment and the piano and the admiring neighbors coming to cakes and coffee, and her family: Anna and Reuben and Klara and Felix, dead by now, dead by now. When I passed her on the street her mouth would lift once—quickly—a parody of a smile, then set again. I wouldn't smile either.

3.

Mami, I swear, we were just skating! Me and Moira. Down the block. No, really! Right in front of the house almost.

Of course I heard them right. They yelled "Kike" and "dirty Jew." And they threw stones at us, at me and Moira.

No, I'm not crying cause they called me Jew. No! Don't you see? Oh, you don't understand anything. The Irish kids from our church, they called us names and threw stones at us. Cause we were Jews. Oh, you know what I mean. They stoned us, Mami! They stoned us.

4.

Asleep, I too am escaping Germany with my new baby in my arms, slipped into a pillowcase for a bunting. Asleep I'm in a crowd of refugees making for the border with Moira and her mother and father, her handsome brother. My baby is small like all the babies in my dreams, small enough to fit in the palm of my hand, so I push it deep into the pillowcase to keep it safe. It's the same dream every time, a long dream of jostling in the crowd and hiding behind bushes or in abandoned buildings from soldiers and policemen and border patrols and finally stopping for the night in a dark field, feeling inside the pillowcase for my tiny child.

Help! It's gone! It's out there somewhere. Help me for god's sake! Help! I run screaming into the crowd, against the inexorable current of fleeing people. I beat on their breasts to make them let me through.

5.

The Bronx has become latinized. I hardly recognize it. In my church where Polish priests and Irish nuns ruled the praying part of my life, a South American priest baptizes children who whimper in Spanish. Out in front, in the cobbled park on what once used to be street and pavement, kids play and chatter at each other in borinquen o dominicano. Down the block at a Mondale rally they hand out leaflets to a salsa beat.

Why am I sad? I'm in my element. It's the others are strangers here, not me, not now, not any more. But I look at the old Synagogue turned into a Christian chapel with a huge sign above the door cut into the corner of the dark brick building, La Roca Eterna, and I'm sad. The Jews are gone. My friends—Lorna and Moira and Jake and Irma and their mothers and fathers and sisters and brothers—and my enemies, the yentas who sat out the summers in front of my stoop and stalked every step of my adolescence.

And Brooklyn, too, where small Puerto Rican shops punctuate the old Jewish barrio. I walk to Brighton Beach Avenue to get milk and find leche, queso, papas fritas. I feel traitorous. I don't want them here. In the old days it was like traveling to another land to go there from the Bronx. I'd get on the elevated at the Intervale stop and go for an hour or more and come down the long flight of steps to land right in front of Mrs. Stahl's Knishes. Yiddish in the streets, Yiddish-flavored English everywhere, and store after store with Hebrew lettering, with Jews selling fruit and meat and groceries and candy, cleaning your clothes, serving your food.

The knish place is still there selling knishes in every flavor: potato (that goes without saying), and cabbage and kasha and cheese and apple and strawberry. Though not the ones I made in Chicago one year, with (forgive me!) pork, and raisins and garbanzos and green Spanish olives, the insides of pasteles, in fact. I want a pure Jewish neighborhood to return to but I make Puerto Rican knishes in Chicago, make Morales blintzes in the mountains of Maricao, make my Jewish chicken soup with cilantro and oregano, raise Jewish-Puerto Rican-American children on aceite de oliva and kosher pickles, pasta de guayaba and pirozhni, empanadas and borscht mit sour cream.

6.

Sitting on the terrace of a restaurant in Vermont—what a lovely place. I see the hills over the roofs of the buildings across the street. There are pigeons of every shade of gray and white, brown and white, roosting on the church steeple. Inside, someone is softly playing the piano. We have a bottle of beer with the cornbread as we wait for supper. Around me, on the oddly assorted wooden chairs, are very very white people in their blond and black and red hair and, like Barbara Cameron feeling very Indian and vulnerable and alone in a room of Wasicu, I think, "I am Puerto Rican and the only one" and my back, like hers, feels unprotected and cold. Then I realize Dick is with me, is Jewish, a red-antiracist-internationalist Jew—the best kind—and that makes two. Maybe more I think, looking again, but at least two.

Trees

to Dick

We have grown together for so long, grown around each other like two old trees in the forest. We were young and close on the forest floor. As we grew our roots grew tangled and swollen together. It takes work to see which roots are which, which root is yours—dark-barked, which root is mine—white and peeling. And when you nearly died, how was I to know I wasn't losing part of me when it is so hard to know now what part of you has become me, cell of my cell, fiber of my fiber. Up here where my head moves with the wind and my leaves flutter and sometimes fall, I know I am I, and I see you over there distinctly you, your trunk large and straight. Mine follows the twists of my growing. But my roots are not my own alone. We have grown our roots together tangled and swollen tight about each other and deep, deep into the ground they go and grow—deep.

Heart Of My Heart, Bone Of My Bone

You were my first grief. From the death of you, so intimate, so much an unexplained event of the universe, I made my first decision to live.

You have no name. That was before names. There were comets plunging into the sun and cells dividing in a frenzy of life too intense, too bright for anything like thinking, but I remember. There was a great space of floating motes and dim light and growing. There were three hearts beating. One, a deep repetition of thunder that was the weather of the universe, a slow rumbling music. And two hearts pitter-pattering, interweaving, fingerlacing, first me then you then me then you, *patta-pun* patta-pun *patta-pun.*

I reconstruct this story from the outside, from knowing what things were, from having names. On the inside, I grew stronger and you grew weaker. I grew and you grew still. I felt your sadness and fear and loneliness without having to interpret signs, read your expressions. The fluids of our bodies mingled in one chemical response: I knew *exactly* how you felt, and never, since then, have I been so completely known.

It was there from the beginning, the thing that was wrong with you. Something I knew but at first was hardly aware of. That grew to trouble me, until slowly I knew that I would lose you. Would be as naked without you as the pulsing electric cord of your spine was naked, unprotected. It was a failure of some part of your body to develop, a loss in the genetic gamble, a part that was necessary and was not there, did not work. *A part that was necessary and is gone.*

On the outside, I read about fetal development, look at pictures, watch *The Miracle Of Life* on TV. I am shivering as I watch: ten days, two weeks, four weeks, seven weeks, twelve weeks, fourteen . . . then nothing. The picture of the sixteen week fetus comes up on the screen, and I feel I have never seen this shape before, pinpointing your death in the shadowy places of my body's memory, a kind of emotional sonogram.

Cell of my cell, bone of my bone, when your heart fluttered and whispered and was still, when you floated passive in the salty water and slowly came undone, frilling and fraying at the edges, becoming strands of protein, disappearing into the walls, the glowing cord my flesh—the stillness that followed was terrible, patta-pun *and nothing*, patta-pun *and nothing*.

You were heart of my heart and my own single heart murmurs and mutters now, an extra beat in each movement, patta-pa-pun, patta-pa-bun, beating "Are you still here? Are you still here?" Trying to find you in the stillness of the house, too big now without you, my own small heart and the thunder above me.

This is all I know: You were the closest being in the world and then you were gone. I have looked for you everywhere, though for years I had no name for the longing, crying in my child's bunk bed at night for someone I missed, not knowing who. Turning over all the stones to find you: If I get sick, too, will you come back? If I promise to die young, will you come back? If I promise never to have another baby close to my heart, will you come back? Patta-pun and no answer. Patta-pun and nothing.

I am a woman rich in brothers. Ricardo, who came when I was two. At my wedding he said, "You were my first coconspirator and soulmate." Partner in all the games of my childhood. Sibling to the wild guava bushes, friend of dogs in every alley of Chicago, companion of my homesickness, with whom I learned the meaning of solidarity.

Alejandro, who was born when I was nearly twelve. The golden treasure we took with us to Chicago, the child of my adolescence, the one I sang to, took mountain climbing, hitchhiked with. The almost-my-son one. The one who reminds me I survived.

I am rich in brothers, rich in love, and still, tiny as my little finger, curled up inside me, is the first seed of myself, wailing to the edges of the empty universe, for my brother, my self, my first lost love.

Tito

April 1985

And so Tito is alive and well in Carrizales. Married to a tiny little wife (according to all the neighbors), and she's already got a big belly. Not dead in some Florida flower field. Not in prison. Not suicidally drunk in a slum apartment in New York or Hartford. Alive in Carrizales and many pounds heavier than when last I saw him.

I was in Liche's store, again, and la nena came in breathless to tell me he was standing outside, in the road, alone. Oh, God! I said under my breath, and Liche said, "No es nada, mija," surprising me with the unexpected reassurance. So I marched out there, friendly and with a good show of cordiality for the onlookers, shook his hand. Kissed his cheek. Congratulated him. Told him I, too, was married. But our eyes were smiling in the half-light of a wooden cabin on a rainy afternoon. That's where we were, and we both wanted to be alone there, talking.

When he offered us a ride home I said no, because it seemed unwise. Every move here is subject to gossip, and I had no desire to make his second wife unhappy with it, so I said no, thinking he would come to Castañer to see me. But he didn't. Maybe he mistook the day, or maybe he thought better of it. I wanted to talk with him in private, out in the dusk with the rising scent of coffee bloom. I wanted that smell in the darkness, and his olivey face across from me with the moths' wings whispering at the edges. To say, "Porque no me escribiste?" To trade information about our lives across the big stone at the edge of the road like small silver coins, an offering to all the years since I was six of bartering with him, a slice of tangerine for the Virgin Mary, a Mary Jane candy, a game of loco, an escapade with the mule, a kiss under the pines. Here: this is what I've made of my time since I saw you last. Now give me yours. What happened after the mushroom sheds of Pennsylvania? Was it hot in Florida? Where did you live with Charo? How did she look? When did you come back? Was it for Haydee or the children, or the smells of home or just nothing to do there? Or did the grimness of poverty in those cities drive you back here where the hunger is at least green? Will I find you here next time? All that to say and ask and only a half-minute in front of the twinkling, note-taking eyes of the store customers.

January 1983

New Year's Eve I saw a man with his face, an American Indian. His high cheekbones and black hair came from a different root than Tito's, with his wild blend of Corsican and Spanish peasant and Taino and escaped African slave and who knows what else, with his green eyes and thick dark hair and olive skin. But the man had Tito's mouth, sensitive the way the leaves of the little ground plant are, quivering under the touch of a finger tip, and held crooked with humor and irony.

January 1985

I keep wanting to know what place it is in me that is moved by Tito. If they are the women in black—his mother, his sisters, my own great-grandmothers—who inhabit my dreams and visions, the folktales of my inner world, he must be another kind of myth. The childhood lover. I imagine him in the dark, but with a glimmer of coffee bloom around him, a quality like the silver of yagrumo leaves in a wind, or the rain of the mountains pattering on banana leaves, the smell of steam rising from hot roads or the sound of jíbaro Spanish. He is boy and world in one. Man and ticket home. Related by childhood.

I have an image of his heart that I carry with me when I'm away from the barrio: a midnight well of sorrow, and in the pit of it, where he can see it each time he is about to hurl himself down that well forever, a scattering of gold coins. His knowledge that I truly love him, will not collude with his dying in any way.

September 1985

This time I have come with Jim. We're standing looking around Rogelio's farm when I see Tito walking toward us with Liche, his drinking buddy. Introductions, handshaking. He's drinking himself deeper and deeper into oblivion. He has just come back from registering his new daughter in Mayaguez. His wife of nine or ten months is resting back at the house. Liche breaks into English and leads Jim (who consents to the ploy) away through the mud to inspect some piece of ground over the hill, out of earshot, so that Tito can say his piece. But his piece is just fragments of old records, tidbits of flattery and flirtation. I have to ignore the words, the cumbersome phrases that are the only way he knows to tell me how I matter to him. I have to ignore the words and watch his hands, ignore the smile, twisted up now into what he imagines is seductiveness, and watch his hands and his eyes. His eyes still remember the rain and farther back, before the rain, the wild leaps we took off the big boulder into the fragrant heaps of soft green fern. I use my marriage to make him shut up. He says, "Está bien. . .voy a respetar." We look at each other and talk about his building a house for me and Jim and look again and laugh. Home in Jim's arms at the parador I cry for a while, then lie still, listening to the coquís. With Jim. Who understands me when I speak. Who listens to the roosters and watches my face to understand their language. Whose heart is a river of gold. All night I sleep on the balance point, where all my worlds meet.

Memory

It's July, it's hot, the mosquito females bite me for the blood to feed their young, and I itch, madly at first, mildly all summer. All summer I am in contact with myself: touching, scratching, drying my sweat, my hand on my thigh, on my neck, reaching for my back. All summer stray breezes on my nipples, or the itchy sweat from my breast's resting place trigger my body's memory. All summer my body remembers. And this sun is the one on Caja de Muertos twenty years ago when it lay desertlike and dry on sand and scrub and skin. And this itch is the one I scratched the summer I was fourteen, when I first followed Jean Valjean thru the sewers of Paris, the one that plagued me while I proudly returned the fat book to the still, hot air of Hunt's Point library, finished, in two weeks, to the librarian's astonishment. This sweat is my sweat in the small end room I shared with my ten-year-old sister in that first-floor apartment in the Bronx: one window, and that behind the door and nowhere for the air to go if ever it stepped in. This cool breeze on my calf is the same one that slid between the metal slats of the fire escape, past my feet and around the pillow I sat on, small and young, quiet and still, because I could see down all six stories of metal platforms and metal steps to the concrete yard below. Only the heat baking the tarred roof above my bedroom, only my mother's hand, kept me there stealing a summer breeze, tasting it dangerously.

All my childhood summers smelled of concrete, of asphalt melting, of the sound of quarreling coming from the windows next door, of chairs in front of the stoop and neighbors gossiping, of sticky bus seats, of sunburn carried home from the beach, like seashells, all the long hours of subway to my room.

Except for one that tasted of seasick and salt at first, then humidity like a layer of cream on my skin, and strangers I was told were kin, and Spanish always Spanish, and no English anywhere, not even on the streets, cousins with strange ways, river bathing and fruit on trees, metal roofs and wooden floors, and the lovely smell of stewed beans simmering on Yeya's stove.

I was in Naranjito, in my father's dreams, in my mother's stories, and she was young like me, skinny, barefoot, riding bareback in the special heat of the Naranjito hills, drinking milk frothing warm from the cow, too rich for me. Oh! And I ran into the storm of raindrops pounding my hair flat, my skirts flat, ran under the cold blows of the waterspout until gooseflesh drove me in. Mami danced in the water and mocked at me and grandmother scolded, scrubbing me red with the towel, muttering at her, "¡Niña loca! ¡No se mata por te'tadura que e'!," kissing my head warm.

My father hides in the coffee grove from the switch aimed at his butt and ankles. Will they catch him now? Please not, for just today he is my age. He'll hide in the ferns with me and show me where the snakes are if I give him my penknife. He'll peel me an orange. He'll take me to his tree and pick me a mangotín.

I will run barefoot just this once, run wild like any títere in the hills of Puerto Rico, bathe in the creek past the pasture with my mother, make mud pies with my aunts, steal tangerines with my daughter, play house with her and Tita, sprawl on the cool tiles with my son and draw ships and soldiers. Just this once I will grow up among the wide green leaves of the plantain, under the shiny coffee leaves and in the dark green spaces beneath, my feet stained pink by the red mud, my skin dark from the noon sun. I will taste the sweetness at the pit of the red hibiscus bloom with a child's tongue, make a whistle from the orange-flowered brucál, suck the sweet guamá. I will jump from the tall rock into the springy ferns below, jump with them all, into the green of their summers again and again.

A Child's Christmas In Puerto Rico

Christmas day was the least of it then, when I grew wild on the mountainsides of Indiera, ranging the coffee farms and filling my skirt with stolen tangerines. Gifts must wait for the Three Kings on their plodding camels to pass wearily through our corner of the world on their way to Bethlehem and stable their beasts at our little offerings of green grass and pine needles. Meanwhile it was the dry season and we sat outdoors, in the yellow light that spilled from the kitchen while Tito Cruz from across the road slipped down to the store where the old men drank their shots of Don Q from paper cups and fetched back Cheo's cousin from Sábana Grande. And he appeared, melting suddenly into the circle of light. "Get him a chair," yells my mother and pours him a little red glass of the best while he tunes his guitar. I remember verse after verse, like dark birds rising from his quiet face with an echo of the moorish troubadours in the high sing-song of the Andalucian peasant and the black cane cutter from Angola all mixing, somewhere far away in his jíbaro blood while nearby, just across the valley, dogs barked at the shadows of the coffee branches skittering in the moon.

But Noche Buena the noise rose from every corner and hollow of the mountains, with the green and red jeeps roaring up and down the roads and Lencho Perez arguing with his wife about the basting of the pig that his son had butchered that morning, the pig that Tita and I had fed orange peels to all fall in the pen on the hill, careful always to walk on the uphill side to keep our shoes clean. All afternoon the pig turned in the pit, and the little boys fought for a chance at the crank, poking to see if it was done, until Chinita la de Ada pulled on its ear and it came off in her hand. Now it was night and the pig was carved into heaps of garlic-pepper-and-oregano-smelling slices, everyone diving for the bits with skin on them, with the smell of arroz con dulce in the oven and huge pots of rice and gandules steaming on top of the stove.

Best of all Spanish turrón and dulce de everything, quivering slabs of candied orange, mango, guava, coconut being sliced with cheese, until outside the bright house there was only soft light brushing the dark hills and the chickens' feathery shuffling under the orange tree, while the pigeons on the porch hummed softly to themselves in their wire cage.

Late, late in the night, sleepy children were bundled into blankets and the jeeps roared off into the scented dark. The road swayed in the headlights, and an owl swung like a brown pendulum across our path. Dogs' eyes lit up red at the roadside, and we thought they were unheard of beasts from the middle-of-the-night.

Down in the cities the fat jovial gringo in the red suit was pushing out the old men on their wise steeds. He spoke better English and had contacts in New York. Some people said he had a brother-in-law in the government. Blonde dolls and GI Joes poured into the small towns and came by mail even to backwaters like ours. Nowadays, my younger cousins wait for Santa with tinsel trees in their living rooms and unwrap Barbie dolls and machine guns and Three Chipmunks Christmas records and never hear the song rise into the dark air filled with the velvet flight of bats, or see the first light pour down the red hill while all the world sleeps it off and the church bells ring in the muffled dawn.

Doña Carmelita

Doña Carmelita is never asleep. When I walk to school in the morning she's out hanging the laundry on our fence to dry. If I get up very early to see a world without birds or people, where the lizards are still asleep on the undersides of branches, she'll be sitting there on her porch, sorting beans with quick, constant motions of her fingers. In the half light I can see her high cheekbones and black, black eyes, her black cotton-silk hair twisted up in a knot behind her head. As I come home she'll be sweeping dust from the boards or heating cafe con leche over a blue flame in her dark kitchen. When she smiles at me, I'm glad she and I are the only ones awake, because her eyes say that we, she and I, know something worth knowing. Sometimes the twist of her smile reminds me of the eucalyptus tree where the last hurricane splintered the wood. It's already bursting with new leaf.

Doña Carmelita's garden is a magic place, full of cans. The cans are shallow, square cookie cans and tall Sultana cans with a woman lying on her side in harem clothes, all yellow and red, and big tomato sauce cans with the paper peeled off them. Each can is set in its own place, and doña Carmelita sweeps the bare ground between them until it's as clean as the wooden floors of her house. They are planted with geraniums, vergüenza with its green and pink and purple leaves, some plain, some ruffled, and alegría from the cool mountainsides, yerba buena to heal all hurts, clumps of daisies, and a plant with silvery, furry leaves. At the end of the garden is a grapefruit tree with fat, sweet grapefruit that taste like the moon when Tita and I pull them from her mother's tree and break them open on the stones. Sweet and bitter and full of indirect light, pale, golden and immense.

Last week Charo ran away with Güilo. I used to watch her tossing raw rice into the air and catching it in her mouth as she walked slowly back behind the house to feed the pigs. Tita says it's because she's pregnant and gets antojos. She tells me their mother was twelve when she got married. Only two years older than me, says Tita. Charo is the most beautiful girl I have ever seen. She has wide cheekbones and smooth cafe-con-leche skin and dark, almond eyes, and brown, silky hair to her shoulders. I want to touch her face, to put the palms of my hands over her eyes. I love to watch the way she sways slowly as she walks, the slow lazy-looking walk of country women. I practice walking that way when I'm alone, letting my sandals slap against my heels. I want her to stay in the house across the road forever, but now she's run off and I won't see her any more. She was one week under fourteen.

"My mother had fourteen."
"Fourteen! You lived with fourteen kids in your house?"
"No, boba! Some of them left before I was born. The oldest ones are forty years old and have kids and everything."
"You have nieces and nephews?"
"Yeah, and some of them are older than me, too. Tata is twelve. I don't like my uncles, though. They're always telling me what to do. Always talking about God and sin and how they should beat us more. My nieces don't mind me, either, and they should. Soy su tía!"

One of Tita's nieces is visiting. Doña Carmelita's grown sons and daughters are in the house. Don Miguel is very sick. Whenever Tita's niece jumps and skips and plays in the road, Tita looks very severe and says sharply, "Respeta! Your grandfather is dying." Mami tells me it's because of his liver and has something to do with drinking so much rum and beating everybody up. I'm glad he's sick. I hope he dies, so he won't beat up Tita and Tito anymore. Doña Carmelita's face looks tired all the time.

Don Miguel is dead. Misi Pradero took the whole fifth grade class up to doña Carmelita's house and made us walk by his coffin. It's the first time I've ever been inside their house. Tita never comes inside mine, either. We stand out in the road and call to each other to come play. Don Miguel looks very small, and I'm surprised. He was always so big, sitting on his porch, frightening his family, but now that he's dead, he's a very small man. I wonder if he'll go on shrinking under the ground and eventually disappear. Is that how the dead become dust? He's lying in a box with white satin ruffles in it like a basinette. His face looks like silly putty. Tita says her mother and her have to go to church every day for nine days and say prayers and light candles. The velorio will last three days. All the relatives come. They drink and make noise and talk and laugh late into the night. When I look out my window toward their house I can see lights and people moving. There are lots of cars parked in the road, and I know Tita won't be out to play until they're gone.

The next time I see doña Carmelita I am shocked. She's happy. I thought she would be sad, listless, bent with grief. Her eyes are bright black and sparkly, as if they were full of fresh raindrops on a hot day. She wears the black dress every day now. I know she will never take it off again. She will wear black for the rest of her life to make up for the sparkle.

Happiness Is A Coquí

*A coquí is a small Caribbean tree frog named after
the sound it makes. Coquís fill the Caribbean night
with music. The one I write about is a species that
lives in El Yunque, the national rain forest of Puerto Rico.*

Happiness is a coquí in my heart
Singing its six swift piercing notes
It fills my chest with hot sharp sounds
That pour out through my skin
Worn to a whistle.

Happiness is a coquí in my heart
Shooting its six sweet beats into my skull
The sound ricochets between the bony walls
and then grows slow,
Worn to a whistle.

The coquí sits quite still now,
Golden green and flattened low on the muscled floor
When it sings again it will quiver with the strain
Of forcing such loud music from an instrument so small.

My throat will quiver too.
I am not used to joy in my heart
Not used to a coquí,
A small live bit of the rain forest,
Lodged firmly in my right ventricle,
Taking enough comfort from that dark moist place
To sing: I'm home, I'm home, I'm home.
Coquí! Coquí!
Coquí quí quí quí quí.

Gardens

Carmelita

Doña Carmelita asks me to give her lessons in Spanish or English. She offers to pay me two dollars an hour. I say, let's do a trade instead. Teach me to garden. She says O.K., come with me. She takes me behind her house to the bare earth. She picks it up with both hands and lets it trickle between her fingers, over and over. Do this, she says. The first step in making the soil fertile, she tells me, is to love it.

Leah

My great-grandmother Leah stands before me, her image more clear and present than any photograph. She shows me her life. She says, "See?, I am one of those immigrants, those refugees you are all the time thinking so much about." I see images of her leaving places and people and things and landscapes behind her. She says, "You want to know gardens? Let me show you gardens!" She shows me her house in Brooklyn and her children growing up around her, and Pop. "You think it matters so much, where you plant, who you have children with. It doesn't matter so much. What matters is how you grow them, how you love them. You can make a garden anywhere, with anything, anyone. The secret is not to leave it behind you, always to plant . . . then always you have a garden. You take it everywhere, then wherever you are, you are in your own garden!"

The Earth

I am standing facing Jim on the rich dark soil that extends out as far as the horizon in all directions, here and there clumps of dark green trees. I am barefoot, and I feel the earth under my feet. From the soles of my feet, roots grow down into the earth, deeper and deeper. Very deep. A voice behind me says: "The most sacred thing you can do with the earth is to sink roots into it."

Wedding Poem

for Ricardo and Paula

Here is the heart of the Northland, wide brown earth
where the names of towns glow like sudden wildflowers in the grass:
Redwing, Stillwater, Spring Valley, Blooming Prairie, Richnewland.
Everything is fertile: the fish, the deer, the corn
and the cornsilk children, the transplanted, immigrant crop.

Great crossroads.
The river runs south, the farmworkers move north.
East and west the railroads, lakeports, highways
rush away with the wealth of the land, bring new and hungry hands.
At the center of four points, a meeting ground.
Those who come sink their fingers into the soil, let it change them.
They roof their houses with sod
and live out the winter under its roots.
In the spring they stand out under the sky with new names.

To this lake-studded platter of black soil, my brother came,
feet of red Caribbean clay,
Afro-Spanish voices hoarse in his dreams, or sweet as falling rain,
eyes like the island dawn, gentle and bright, hands
that feel for the texture of things—
came walking north into the colors of this weather:
purple thundered green summers, blue-white winters,
autumns copper, gold, wine red, smoke blue,
the murky river running south
and the corn-colored hair of its children,
their black, Anishinabe eyes, their brown migrant hands,
gesturing.
Came to their palette, sat down,
and painted a map of his heart on a white deer hide.

Walked north
to a midwestern woman, strong and fresh,
eyes that push back the horizon
hands that piece color, shape words,
measure and make
fingers to knead bread or hold a rock
that catch the gestures of   ¡Ay, mi madre!
SI SE PUEDE   Patria Libre   Negro. . .ven acá
like stitches of knitting, and learn to twist her blue thread
through and around them.

Raise now the wedding roof, cornfield and cafetal
Stamp down the floor with bare feet
made smooth by all the miles they have walked to meet here.
Gather this house from the harvest of seasons spent
hang the windows with seed and leaf
garnish the sills with fruit.

When the fire has fed us and we all go home
let the flames die down into the nest of night.
Let there be only the red heart of the fire, let the white ash
fall away in a song of braided limbs
and the white stars hunt the dawn down the four winds.
Then, while they're sleeping, open and breathing,
let a new day turn, turn,
into their waiting hands.

Flowering
In
The
Dust
Of
The
Road

I Am What I Am

I am what I am and I am U.S. American   I haven't wanted to say it because if I did you'd take away the Puerto Rican but now I say go to hell   I am what I am and you can't take it away with all the words and sneers at your command   I am what I am   I am Puerto Rican   I am U.S. American   I am New York Manhattan and the Bronx   I am what I am   I'm not hiding under no stoop   behind no curtain   I am what I am   I am Boricua as Boricuas come from the isle of Manhattan and I croon sentimental tangos in my sleep and Afro-Cuban beats in my blood and Xavier Cugat's luke-warm latin is so familiar and dear   sneer dear but he's familiar and dear   but not Carmen Miranda who's a joke because I never was a joke   I was a bit of a sensation   See! here's a real true honest-to-god Puerto Rican girl and she's in college   Hey! Mary   come here and look she's from right here   a South Bronx girl and she's honest-to-god in college now   Ain't that something   who wouda believed it   Ain't science wonderful or some such thing   a wonder a wonder.

And someone who did languages for a living stopped me in the sub-way because how I spoke was a linguist's treat   I mean there it was yiddish and spanish and fine refined college educated eng-lish   and irish which I mainly keep in my prayers   It's dusty now   I haven't said my prayers in decades but try my Hail Marrrry full of grrrace with the nun's burr with the nun's disdain   it's all true and it's all me   do you know I got an English accent from the BBC   For years in the mountains of Puerto Rico when I was twenty-two and twenty-four and twenty-six   all those young years   I listened to the BBC and Radio Moscow's English english an-nouncers announce and denounce and then I read Dickens all the way through three or four times at least and then later I read Dick-ens aloud in voices and when I came back to the U.S. I spoke mock-Dickens and mockBritish especially when I want to be crisp efficient I know what I'm doing and you can't scare me   tough   that kind   I am what I am and I'm a bit of a snob too   Shit! why am I calling myself names   I really really dig the funny way the British

speak   and it's real it's true   and I love too the singing of yiddish sentences that go with shrugs and hands and arms doing melan-
choly or lively dances   I love the sound and look of yiddish in the
air   in   the   body   in   the   streets   in   the   English   language   nooo   so what's new   so go by the grocer and buy some
fruit   oye vey   gevalt   gefilte fish   raiseleh   oh and those
words   hundreds of them dotting the english language like raisins in the bread   shnook and shlemiel   zoftik   tush   shmata
    all those soft sweet sounds saying sharp sharp things   I am
what I am and I'm naturalized Jewish-American   wasp is foreign
and new but Jewish-American is old shoe familiar   shmata familiar
and it's me dears it's me   bagels blintzes and all   I am what I
am   Take it or leave me alone.

Spring Fever?

You,
You're like a crocus, like a sugar maple
Your juices ooze in the tepid sun
Pushing against your flesh
Out to your eyes your hair your fingertips
Leaving you pulsing and vulnerable
To the ever returning frost.
And all on this faint promise of the warmth to come.

Not I.
I need steady warm breezes to unfreeze my blood
I need to sink my chilled bones in a soup warm sea
I need to soak my brittle flesh in the burning sun.

Oh! I will be a lizard and sit on a sun hot stone
I want to lie flat, lie lifeless
A cold and scaly sponge
Lie belly close to the dull rough stone
And twitch my tail in low, slow, lazy circles
Eyes closed
Limbs still
Soaking
Waiting
For the strong, slow, baking heat
To stir me into life.

No, Camus

*I took French in college and the first book I read
all the way through in French was* La Peste *by Camus. The novel is set in Oran, a city in North Africa on the Mediterranean that turns its back on the
sea. Spring in Oran was not a burgeoning. Spring
in Oran, said Camus, was something bought and
sold in the marketplace.*

In the South Bronx
spring was not available for sale.

The flowers in the florist shop
have been there all winter
They're not flowers of a season—I doubt they even grow
They're manufactured creatures
bought to bribe a woman
or apologize for our health at a hospital bedside.

Between the squares of Bronx sidewalks
there is more cracked cement
not brave blades of grass.
And on the empty lot there are tin cans
and the dog shit of a whole neighborhood
no weeds
no trees
Not even the hardy city specimen
that leafs out each year
into dust that settles down so densely
that it goes grey before it's green.

Year round indoors
there is a plant or two
usually snakeplant
an iron plant rusty and upright
persisting without growing
in the cracked earth of neglected flower pots in unhappy schoolrooms.
Hard to imagine
that it owns the sonorous name of Sansievaria
that it grows lushly and freely in the tropics
takes over gardens and roadsides
that it flowers in long white fragrant spikes above proud stiff leaves.

No, Camus.
Spring in the South Bronx is only the loosening of coat buttons
and the slight upward lift of the down-turned faces
from their winter positions.

Sketch

I look forward to it every day, to the starlings' early evening flight past our building. The sound of them came, before the moving shifting black mass made its way home to the underpass at 125th Street by the river, the underpass it was foolishness to pass under, or park at, for the night. They would fall on the rooftops like rain, and roost on the copings, the antennae, the chimneys, alight and fly off and shuffle and chatter and shift and sit and fly up and chirp and sit again. The dead brick out my window came alive with them and I'd leap up for my pencil ("Where did I leave my pad?") and sketch roughly, quickly, trying to capture the manyness of them, their busyness, the way the pattern of shifting bird filled the roof-edged, window-pierced brick landscape that was all I had to replace the banana plants, flamboyanes, hibiscus, avocados, and fern trees I had left behind . . .

. . . and the moist undergrowth I would push through silently to where I'd heard a pájaro bobo—the lizard cuckoo—its raucous cry a harsh *khah khah khah.* I had to move quickly to catch the large bird's downward flight, to watch it climb up the grapefruit tree, hop up branch by branch to the top where it would launch itself out again, and down, khahing loudly, to the next tree. There it would sit, twisting its snakelike neck to preen, to search its surroundings, its long horizontally striped tail hanging black and white, black and white, straight below its rusty breast. I would hold my pad in my hand and draw the neck lines, the large beady eye, the moving tail.

But even here in this brick and cement insane asylum of a city I could reach out and reel in some bird lines, a bird shape wrapped in paper for the winter, to feed my hunger for the joy, the winged aliveness that had shot through me— eye to hand to paper—pinned to the creamy page.

Sweet Language

Sweet language
Crisp tasty words left too long and
Turned soft and heavy like the baby at my breast
Turned vinegary like my milk souring
Till worms tunneled their fruitiness and fed on it
Metamorphosed to flies.
Others
Stretched and grew
Others
Fed on the winey mash of my spent talent.

I Recognize You

I recognize you. Spitting out four, five, six-syllable English words, your tongue turning a tight grammatical sentence, flipping adjectives and adverbs into line faster than you can say *Oxford Unabridged Dictionary* and pinning all of it in place with commas, colons, semicolons, and parentheses.

You were the one I couldn't beat at spelling bees, the other girl who got *A* in grammar two semesters in a row. You're the one who went on to college, or maybe didn't, but took classes after work, who reads and reads and worries whether you're reading enough or the right thing.

I know without meeting you that you're working class, or a woman of color, or an immigrant, or child of immigrants. That you keep your mama language for the kitchen, hardly ever pronounce it in public, never on the written page.

You're proud. You've done this by yourself, or with your family behind you. And I'm impressed. You can make the English language roll over, bark on command, sit up and beg, you—who were raised on spuds, grits, rice, or tortillas.

But I'm sad, too. For the English language robbed of the beat your home talk could give it, the words you could lend, the accent, the music, the word-order reordering, the grammatical twist. I'm sad for you, too, for the shame with which you store away—hide—a whole treasure box of other, mother, language. It's too rough-mannered, you say, too strange, too exotic, too untutored, too low class.

You're robbing us, robbing the young one saying her first sentence, reading her first book, writing her first poem. You're confirming her scorn of her cradle tongue. You're robbing her of a fine brew of language, a stew of words and ways that could inspire her to self-loving invention.

And you're robbing yourself. . . no, we're robbing ourselves, of self-ness, of wholeness, of the joys of writing with *all* our words, of the sound of your Mama's voice, my Papa's voice, of the smell of the kitchen on the page.

I Am The Reasonable One

I am the reasonable one. I am the one you can say your spite to, the one you can ask the venomous questions. It's so hard to say your contempt of these loud, dirty, emotional people if you're white, rational, and liberal. Your self-expression is so limited by your self-repression, and what can you do with your bile?

I am the reasonable one and, best of all, I am your friend. We have sat together, talked together, given and received support, touched hands, touched cheeks. You know me to be kind, to be thoughtful.

You know me to be reasonable, to be rational. You know me to be almost white, almost middle class, almost acceptable. You can count on me, hopefully, to answer quietly, reasonably, and if I don't, you can say, "Don't take it personally." You can ask, "You're not angry with me?" You can trust me, nearly, to answer "No."

I am the one Puerto Rican you can ask, "Why don't they learn English?" And what I answer is full of love and understanding of all those people, your ancestors included, who were forced by the acculturated jingoist migrants of a previous generation to abandon their languages—yiddish, irish, chinese, japanese, tagalog, spanish, french, russian, polish, italian, german—to give birth to your acculturated jingoist selves.

I am the one who hears it all. You can speak freely about "them," about the lower classes, about puertoricans, about blacks, about chinese. When you lower your voice to ask about them, to talk about them, you don't lower it to exclude me. You know you can tell me.

I am the one you can say "people like us" to, meaning white middle class women who are fine, who are right, whose ways are the only ways, whose life is the only life.

And if I say, "not me"—oh, and I do say, "not me"—you do not need to listen. Surely! You can pooh-pooh my stubborn clinging to being different. You know me better than I know myself. You know I am white like you, english-speaking like you, right-thinking like you, middle-class-living like you, no matter what I say.

And through this all, I have ever been the reasonable one, never wanting to betray myself, to become before your eyes just exactly what you despise: a loud and angry spik, cockroaches creeping out of my ears, spitty spanish curses spilling out of my wet lips, angry crazy eyes shooting hate at you. All victims of all racist outrages look like that in your eyes, like your own evil personified, the evil you participate in, condone, or allow.

But now I tell you reasonably, for the last time, reasonably, that I am through. That I am not reasonable anymore, that I was always angry, that I am angry now.

That I am puertorican. That under all that crisp english and extensive american vocabulary, I always say *mielda*. I say *ai mami, ai mami* giving birth. That I am not like you in a million ways that I have kept from you but that I will no more.

That I am working class and always eat at the only table, the kitchen table. That taking things is not always stealing; it's sometimes getting your own back, and walking around in my underwear is being at home.

And I am angry. I will shout at you if you ask your venomous questions now, I will call you racist pig, I will refuse your friendship.

I will be loud and vulgar and angry and me. So change your ways or shut your racist mouths. Use your liberal rationality to unlearn your contempt for me and my people, or shut your racist mouths.

I am not going to eat myself up inside anymore. I am not going to eat myself up inside anymore. I am not going to eat myself up inside anymore.

I am going to eat you.

The Century Plant

For years it sat, immobile, a weighty bouquet of greening spear points, threatening trespassers, pricking passersby. I circled round it warily, and then, while I blinked, it bloomed! A giant asparagus of a spike shot out, shot up, reached up, pushed into the air, burst into the sky—and stopped. Then opened up, branches like umbrella spokes from which hung, first green flowers like bells, then leafy bulblets that dived into the ground, heavy end first, to bury themselves in the red brown clay and start again.

Life blossomed along the inflorescence, lizards sunned and mated, insects buzzed, birds rushed, flew, pecked, preened, hung from branches, bit at flies ants spiders. They chattered, scolded, threatened, sped for home.

Up, on the tippy-top of this circus of a plant, sometimes a bird would come to sit and stare. Up there, forty feet above the three-thousand-foot hill I lived on, it could rest, look down and around the island, tune in on everyone, on anything to sing home about. And at the foot, where the thick sword leaves turned gold in the low light of the falling sun, I sat on an old lawn chair taking in the bird taking in the sights.

One bird, because only one at a time could sit on that pinpoint growing tip that had pulled the whole show out of the ground and out of the spiky eightfoot circumference usurping a path and half a garden bed. And only ten years after it had been planted, not a century at all.

What The Eye Of The Hurricane Sees

Heart's Desire

Sometimes wanting
makes my heart shrink to a small hard stone:
you love me in your own ways, beyond my control
and nothing
        seems to end my hunger.

The worst thing about oppression—
this was said to me by a Guatemalan Indian, an exiled guerrillero,
a man carrying nothing but his shirt—
is what happens to our desires, how they shrink to no more
than a slice of bread, a roof.

Now I am angry with years
of stunting my appetite to fit the meal
shrinking my heart to sit conveniently
in someone's back pocket
pruning my desires into a seemly shape, so nothing untidy
will spill over the garden wall
no wild blossom reaching to the stars
no branches heavy with fruit, bent to the ground.

The arm, it says in this woman's book,
        in the end shapes itself to the cast.

So yes, I tell you,
I am insatiable.
My life depends on it.

Letter To A Compañero

Dear Compañero:

Let's talk about solidarity, then. You name it in every tight spot, as if it were your credit card for drawing on the Revolution, a people's version of American Express. As if it were an endless obligation to surrender the goods. Now, when I confront you with having lied to me, once again you take solidarity's name in vain. As if it were a social obligation, like inviting the neighbors to dinner because our dog tore up their lawn. As if it were a tax on our progressiveness, to compensate for the blood tax our government levies to sink its iron claws into your people's backs. As if it were a duty, like giving a quarter to save a pagan baby.

I say solidarity is knowing the future is long and wide, with room for everyone on earth to enter. I say it's taking the long view of the job. Helping you onto the wall, so you can reach down and pull me up. Lifting you into the tree, so you can shake down peaches for two. That solidarity is a two-way street, fires burning at both ends, and the only well at the middle. I tell you my country. . . but you don't let me speak of my country. You tell me another piece of your story. You tell me your blood is burning and you have no time.

You have come here, men mostly, from the ironclad nations, exiled out of prison cells of torture, or living like you, in the nooks and crannies of your country, temporarily out on tour and going back to who knows what consequences. There are the ones like Paco, in jail at sixteen, exiled at nineteen, half his friends dead, now eight years later suddenly hurling a hamburger at the floor yelling "I hate this damn country!" There are the ones like you, temporarily out from under, whispering it's been a decade since I could walk down a street saying my own name, talking about politics. Even here, I can't stop myself from looking over my shoulder.

I think about what you carry through all the work, the benefits and speeches, the bulletins and campaigns: the people killed, the memory of torture and fear, the anguish of so much loss. I think of your desperation for someone to touch your wounds so you can finally scream, hold your sorrow, so you can shake and weep, and how you seek it the way you have learned to, settling for another kind of touching, always disappointed, always looking for more.

I think about the word *solidarity* and who carries it, the day to day work of it. Women mostly. Mostly white women, many of them activists for the first time, their hearts flung wide open by these stories, crying over each bit you tell them, taking up your nightmares, wanting to heal you, free you, do anything to end the pain, comforting you in the way they have learned to, opening their arms and bodies. Falling in love with your history when they don't know or treasure their own. Intimidated by what you have survived, and minimizing their own survivals. The ones who are wracked with guilt when you accuse them of eating carrot cake while people are dying. Who decide to work harder when you declare you have not had a vacation since the coup and will not rest until liberation, even though they watch you collapse with the flu three times a year. Even when we know it's ridiculous, wracked with guilt, romanticizing the horrors, agreeing not to ask for anything.

So you write to me that I am the compañera of your dreams, the one you have been waiting for. You write the letter five times. You send it to me in Oakland and Amy in New York and Sally in Washington and Dana in San Diego, and you also recite it to Luz, the woman you have been secretly lovers with for the last two years of your marriage to Elena. Elena is the only one I know about. I write back to you asking about Elena, explaining how I feel about these situations, and you write back praising my honesty which you tell me shines like a bright light through the page, saying you are divorced now because she was not a true revolutionary, not a New Woman like me, and that you want to walk beside me until death and even after. In triplicate. (Dana has lost interest. Amy is just after a fling.) Elated, I write that I will meet you in New York for the concert. There I learn about Amy. When I go to the airport to meet you, I learn about Luz, because she is with you. She and I talk. I show her my letter. She has heard the same words herself. You have assured her there is no one waiting for you here, even though she has known for months that you got letters from California. When we confront you, you say it hurts you more than it hurts us. I am not disarmed. I am mortified. I am furious. I am hurt beyond words. You are humble until I agree to continue my work for your tour. Then you act offended. You say personal problems should not be allowed to interfere with duty.

Now listen to me. I will not walk on one-way streets any longer. Your wound is my wound, (though you don't know that mine is yours), and I do what I can, but the well will run dry. You will use us up. There are women whose first stretching across borders was into your lives. When they discover how you make use of their compassion, they will turn away heartsick, stricken, withering in the freshness of their hope. There are women who were leaders, who worked night and day, defeated not by foreign policy, but by the sexual politics of solidarity, bitter now, unable to work anywhere near you. How dare you speak of the New Woman! We are your richest resource besides your endurance, and you use us like rags to wrap around your pain.

Listen to me. I, too, have a homeland to win. I love this second country of mine. It is more than the belly of a monster. It is more than the claws of an empire. More than Pentagons and CIAs. My country is a rug woven from the rebel threads of a hundred homelands. My country is rich with heroism and honesty. Rich with daring and defiance. Humming with song. No less precious under the weight of its evils than your own. Long after the dictator has fled and the streets are renamed, long after you have found the graves of your missing and taught the children to sing their names, we will be working to free ourselves from the shadows: your battle in this moment is bloodier, more urgent. Ours will be the longer one, the more difficult to win.

Take the name of solidarity from your lips, my brother, my compañero, until you can love each woman and man of my country the way you love the day of your freedom, or the wild flamingos on the salt flats of Antofagasta, or the light of your daughter's eyes. We are not the guilty ones, and we will not shoulder their burdens. Our government is not ours. We do not owe you for their actions. The work we do is for love. We are the light and hope of the U.S. of North America, and if you can hold our lives the way that we've held yours, then each and every one of us will get home.

Double Allegiance

I was torn, quite literally, the tear starting somewhere behind my left ear where my mother whispered duérmete nena to an afro beat when I was a little white-skinned spik with brown cousins cruising in my veins. And it was wrenched from my other ear, the one fed with yiddish-accented english sung in the streets of my adolescence. The raspy sound of cartilage parting from bone distracted me from the conference room where they stood up one after the other, jewish woman or woman of color, black or latina or any of the amazing mixtures of our various diasporas, ripping off sleeves to show the numbers tattooed on the bare skin, numbers passed on with hair color and the urge to hide, or pulling off blouses to bare ancient whip marks down black spines. A workshop, to heal our differences, I'd thought, but the noises were war cries, were competition for the one-down spot, each trying to prove to the other how much more oppressed *she* was, to prove she was the *only* one oppressed.

"Sure," I heard one cut in, "sure you're black and you get shit every day on your dark face, but they never tried to wipe you out, every one of you, every one," and sat down.

"Oh yes," the answer flicked out, "and so you say *history, history*. Something that you heard about, something that happened someplace else to someone else. And then you'll just sashay outa here in your bright white skin, step right over me where I'm getting my dark face ground into the dirt today, you hear, today." Oppression thrown at each others' faces like slaps.

Neither of them heard me ripping, heard my whimper, trying not to cry out loud from pain, heard the other women trying to hold my seams together with kindness.

But I heard two more voices pulling me apart. The first voice, jewish, stinging from this crack slung across her face: *You* can always get a nose job. She spoke:

Hear.

I am frightened. I know I can be boxcarted off, imprisoned shot gassed like my aunt Tessie, like Samuel of the round face. I've worked so hard to shape myself into anglosaxon the way my aunt Tessie shaped herself into aryan into middle class, conforming, accepting. But I know they'll search me out, they'll find me the way they do in my dreams and they will put a yellow star upon my brow.

The second voice, dark skinned, darker than my kin, but close enough for comfort:

If you have a black skin or a brown skin or a yellow skin or a red, that's it, baby. No use worrying about when or where they'll find you. They find me every day. I get it every day. You've got a white skin and you pretend it isn't safety in the street, money in the bank, a leg up in any job, anytime.

Hear me.

I am dark in a racist society and I have no place to hide. Now. This minute. And all the minutes of my life.

Each spoke and then sat down with her hands on her ears while mine tore slowly and painfully. So that I had to go home to sew my-self together with the thread we'd spun, my jewish girl friends and I, made out of our games and fantasies, of tastes of each other's foods and each others tears, of our parent's memories of cities hastily abandoned—Naranjito, Kiev, Munich—of yiddish-spanish accents in our speech, of browning photographs of grandparents we hardly knew, of the feel of our arms around each other. I ran small running stitches up my scalp, small chain stitches down my face, then stopped and wound what thread was left carefully onto the spool. It was about time, I thought, to give part of it away. No, all of it. I can make more.

Bad Communist

I am political in spite of myself. I don't want to do the things I know I have to do, don't want to expose myself to disapproval, to retribution, don't want to go to meetings and demonstrations, distribute leaflets, don't want to ask people for signatures, for money.

I don't do these things as naturally as I breathe, the way I imagine *real* political people do, real communists, real socialists and feminists, real radicals, real troublemakers, real champions of the people. I do them because I know I've got to, because I am convinced it's the only way to make changes, to stop abuses. I do them almost as a last resort. I do them because I've been putting off doing them, avoiding them for months, because finally the necessity has gripped me and overcome my reluctance, my desire for the warmth of my room, for my books, for my people, for the reassurance of my homely habits.

Ever since I first faced hecklers from a soapbox on a New York City street corner in 1949, I've known I was a bad communist. Not a Communist with a capital *C*—a member of a Communist Party—but a communist with a small *c*—a militant, a fighter, a person who will battle injustice everywhere and work for a new society without it. But sometimes in my more forgiving moods, or my more defensive ones, I think we need more communists like me, who remember all too well what the shouting and the fighting is for. The fighting is so people can have what I want, can count on the warmth of their room, can slip into the rhythm of their days. We want to live in peace without the grip of a policeman's hand on the shoulder, the threat of the rapist at the door, without a gun to our ribs, with food and good work to do every day of our lives. I get furious that we can't have that, that people in so many places can't have that. And sad.

These days I am sad and angry all the time. The necessity is so clear, the guns and bombs so obvious, the rapes, arrests, deaths so common, the threat, the hunger so omnipresent. But. . .

I want so badly to rise every morning and write, sit every noon and sew on my quilts, get up every afternoon and walk. I want some of the peace that years of childrearing, years of picketing, leafletting, caucusing, and meeting denied me. I want some of the single-mindedness impossible when there was a house to clean, food to prepare, a mimeograph to fix, children to respond to, factions to conciliate. I pursue it. I'm sitting now with my teacup by my side, the sun rising higher in the sky with every word that slides out of my pen. But...

I feel terrible. Strong-voiced East European Jewish matriarchs of the Left, true fighters, the mentors of my Communist youth, stand before me, arms akimbo, say, "Nu? So when will you get off your tuchus, already?" Please, I plead, just one more day of peace, just one more page.

I'm too old now to expect that I can will myself to become like them. I must accept myself, poor communist that I am. But even I know the time has come. So I answer them: All right, already. Enough. I'm coming. (Oh me, oh my, oh me.) I'm coming!

My Revolution

My revolution is not starched and ironed
    (Stand over the ironing board, wield the hot iron)
It is not ass-girdled and breast-bound
    (Wiggle and worm into it every morning, wiggle and worm out
       of it every night)
My revolution is not white-gloved and white-suited
    (Soak it and scrub it and bleach it. . .and wear it?
      Only with care!)
It's not thick-soled and heavy high-booted
    (Lift the left foot. Down. Now lift the other.)

My revolution is comfortable
    hard-wearing
      long-lasting
        versatile!
I can wear it in the fields
I can wear it to go dancing
      do the dishes
      do the laundry
      see the movie
      do the marching

My revolution is not cut from a pattern, *I* designed it.

It's homemade and hand-crafted
It's got seams to let out
    and hems to let down
      tucks to take in
        darts to take out.

My revolution is comfortable
    hard-wearing
      long-lasting
        versatile!

My revolution fits
So well
Sometimes
I don't know I'm wearing it.

So, when your revolution doesn't fit
                    ain't your size
                    chokes
                    binds
                    climbs up your crotch
                    bites into your breasts
                    or rubs your heels raw

Give it back!
Turn it in!
Ask for a refund!
        and make yourself another
                make one of your very own.

Storytelling

A woman asked me the other day where I get enough stories to tell, how I come up with the stuff. I could tell she was imagining me sitting at my desk scratching my head, waiting for inspiration.

I told her I am an attic stuffed to bursting with other people's stories which, after long enough of pressing outward on the walls of my head, have become my own. I told her I pick up stories in bus stations and on planes, in the newspaper and by eavesdropping in public places. That I pocket them like stones found on a beach. I told her that I grew up inside legends, surrounded by stories of preceding times.

I almost spilled them all right there on the bench. I could have opened the attic door, turned my pockets inside out, and loosed the whole heap of them on to Shattuck Avenue if the bus hadn't come. I imagine them bouncing and rolling all over the sidewalk, between the legs of passers-by.

Stories about César and Jane and Maga,
our predecessors in the house
Jane with the red hair to her hips
and Maga her mother
aristocratic communists from Alabama who wrote leaflets
and agitated and went to jail
and had high tea at four o clock on Sundays and left their mark
on the house and the gardens
(forget-me-nots in the strawberry patch,
dahlias among the tomatoes, gladiolas everywhere),
who gave us a taste for Gilbert and Sullivan
and a hand-stitched Puerto Rican flag made
in the days when it was illegal to own one.
Whose ghosts came to me in a high fever once, and gave me
sound advice.

Stories about the land itself before we lived on it,
and stories about the immigrant ancestors who came from the cold
Russian grasslands and forests
fleeing pogroms and the Tsar's draft:

*great-great-great-grandmother the rabbi's wife who protested because
she was forbidden to be a rabbi herself,*

*great-grandma Leah who told other women about birth control and
abortion and helped organize the seamstresses,*

*great-great uncle Sussman Levinsky who in his days of immigrant
poverty became the father of twins and killed one because he could
not afford to feed two, and years later, when he became more prosperous, adopted a child to take the place of the murdered one.*

And the ones from Andalucía, Spaniards bearing Moorish names,
and the ones from West Africa, their names stolen from
them but their eyes looking out of family portraits,
and the ones who were born in these hills out of the first people
who cultivated the soil, leaving liquid words behind them:
guaraguao, huracán, hamaca, ararú, guarapo, Maricao,
(My home, Maricao)
and stories even before that of the Arawak migration north
up the chain of islands from the warm river valleys,
out of the continent's heart in a legendary past.

*How I was taught to listen to that spine of the island we lived on,
to the land itself for stories. How I knew about the millions of bones
of small coral creatures heaped up under us like the seven circles
of Troy, ruin upon ruin, the seven million cities of coral in an immense undecipherable archeology beneath the floor of our house.*

And the stories told by my own bones
Moure, Hernandez, Sakhnin,
the fables of genetics, the clues hidden in bone structure,
in the tilt of the eyes.
The way we made fun of but also believed
the wild universality of heredity
in my grandmother Lola's accounts of the family:
how every trait was inherited from someone—
not only features, the Morales nose, the Hernandez knees—
but the Hernandez temper, too.
And the Morales tendency to delirium with low fevers,
and the ability to wake up out of deep sleep and know where one is,
a trait the Moure-Diaz side has and the inbred Morales family lacks,
and even the like or dislike of particular foods,
which ancestor liked sweets, who craved their plátano frito done
to just that same degree of crispness.
No one is destitute in her scheme of things, no one orphaned.
Our ancestors keep watch over each morsel of food we eat,
quarreling among themselves about how best to season it.

How I was steeped in history all my early life. Bedtime stories about
Cheng Ho, medieval Chinese navigator plying the routes along the
east coast of Africa in a Chinese boat with sails of brown silk, and
a father who said we had come over, not on the Mayflower, but on
the Wisconsin Glaciation.

My father would walk me along the blurred impressions left in the
hillside from the old Spanish road, Camino Real, the king's road. It
elevated that narrow dip along the mountain's flank into a thing worthy of great expeditions of discovery: Machu Pichu, the Sphinx,
Ozymandias, King of Kings.

*And he told me about the lives of the little red ants and the black
fire ants and the green lizards called Evermani and the brown lizards
with their quick darting and their flickering tails and the tangerine*

colored gekkos who creep along like parodies of stealth and the moths and flies and snails and bats and owls and all the varied animal life in the space we pretended to own.

So that I felt the legends of the midges in the evening air and gasped with them at the swooping shadows of the swallows, and knew the tales of the swallows like a moorish inscription or the verses of Bequer set to guitar and played in the dusk; and knew the stiff, red-winged fables of the hawks whose name is Guaraguao, the high-pitched scream of keeeeeeu that freezes all the scuffling, flitting life of chickens and little birds in the bushes below, gluing them to their shadows, motionless as they wait for death to pass.

And the slow meandering of snails up and down through the wilderness of our garden leaving sticky silvery trails behind them, tacky and gleaming; knew the construction and evolution of each shell, the bands of light and dark, the meaning of those verses.

There is no wonder, I tell the people who ask. I grew up in the lap of a storyteller and the story he told was the world, always reading it to me out loud. Legends, tales, history, tracing the roots of gestures, of structures, of songs, always looking to speak another language.

I am an immigrant. I am always looking for a country, inventing countries I can belong to in the words of a cranky woman on the subway or the sad, defiant eyes of an exiled Chilean, or the story of what happened to each one of you, writing from the fire-edged country of childhood from which I was forced to flee, to which I return in disguise, smuggling out what I can.

In other words, no, I would have said with the stories quivering in front of her face like shimmering dragonflies, I have no trouble finding stories to tell.

I Never Told My Children Stories

I never told my children stories. I said I couldn't make things up. "Go ask your father. He makes things up all the time." Now me—I like the truth. I figured if I ever wrote any stories, they'd be true stories, things that happened to me, the real stuff of life, not all that airy invention.

Of course, that was before I realized how much of my truth was embroidered. No, not embroidered exactly—just remembered in special ways. Before I began thinking of people's truths as the stories they tell about themselves. Oh well, I might as well get personal. Before *I* began seeing *my* truth as the story *I* tell to let you know what I think *I'm* all about, to clue you in on what I think I'm all about, to clue you in on what is *really* happening: how I'm pretty lucky, and about the rotten childhood I had, or how mean people have been to me. You know, these stories are like stage directions in a play, telling you how to do the character.

Zoreida—she sees herself as upright and values her integrity. She dramatizes her life, everything that happens to her, tragic mostly, but comic too. Play her large but with restraint, as if all that energy, all that drama that is her life must be strenuously held in if it's not to explode all over everybody.

See? Drama. It's my sense of drama that made me see the fiction in the telling of my life. Girl, I'm really into those dramatic values, whatever those things are. Heighten a little here, smooth there. Those are irrelevant details and detract from the main point. And oh my! My sense of timing!

That's what made me see I could tell stories, too. Cause if that's what a story is, honey, I'm for it, I'm with it, I'm your woman and here we go!

Of course, now that I'm here and real conscious that I'm going to dramatize and tell a story, I'm all self-conscious and shy. It's one thing

to do it naturally, it's another to sit down in cold blood and dramatize. Go ahead Zoreida, dramatize.

Yeah, perform. "Zoreida, go kiss titi María. Show them your new
shoes. Show them how much you've grown. Show them how well
you play the piano. Do the piece you did for me yesterday. Do a tap
dance, Zoreida. Stand on your head Zoreida. Jump out of the window Zoreida." Fuck it! Why can't they leave little girls alone. You'd
think all we were were wind-up toys you pulled out of the drawer
and set on the floor to amuse the relatives. Nah. I won't perform
on command. I won't. I get angry just thinking about it.

"Act one, scene two." My sister said that. Oh boy—I just remembered
her getting at me with those words. You have to hear the sneer in
them to understand them though. Try it again, real exaggerated, the
way only an eight-year-old can sneer "Act one, Scene two." She'd do
it whenever I got worked up about something. Mean bitch. It was
like feeling anything at all was acting. I guess that's why it took me
so long to see about how I dramatized. If I admitted it, it was like
admitting to my sister that all my feelings were a big act put on just
to impress her. Well, fuck her too.

I probably had to exaggerate to get heard. My sister just sneered,
and my mother was being the tragic heroine of a novela. "Mi vida
es como una novela," she used to say.

A novela is a puertorican soap opera, and shit, they beat your stuff
hollow for drama. I mean they really let themselves go. And they
all talk a fancy kind of Spanish, all hissing with esses and syllables
like a Spanish Shakespeare or something. Not that my mother talked
that way. No, it's just that everything that happened to her was part
of this novela. That there were mustachioed evil men plotting to do
her wrong and shifty-eyed women jealously trying to trip her up and
really heavy things befell her and she foiled them all and rose white-
breasted and triumphant out of heaps of ashes again and again. Why,
just going to the grocer was fraught! She dressed up for it like for

a first night—catch her running across the street in her bata and a naked face! And if he gave her a special price, her smile hinted at ancient liaisons and secret passions.

No wonder I was into telling the truth, trying to tell the strict truth, and who me? tell stories?

Now that I told you about my mother and my sister, I should tell you about my father. And how he fit into all this—but I don't know. It's still hard for me to get a perspective on him. He's *too* real. Most of that is my mother's doing. She dramatized him to hell-and gone, and I drank it all in. I believed every word and if there were villains in my mother's life, my father was top villain, a sort of Moriarty to her Holmes, the evil genius who was plotting to do her in, kill her.

I don't know how many times she'd tell us that he would kill her, mostly when me and my sister said, "Leave him, divorce him." She'd say—heavy voice, scared face, eyes darting sideways—"He'd shoot me!"

Why just the other day I realized for the first time that my mother was over seventy, and she never did get killed. What a gyp!

Not that I wanted her dead. Far from it. I took it on myself to keep her alive. No, it's just that I spent my childhood—my life—being terrorized for no good reason. It's just the novela taking over again. "Mi vida es como una novela." My life is like a soap opera. Nah. It doesn't sound right in English, it sounds comic. It hasn't got the pizzazz, the dramatic power, the believability of the Spanish: eyes slightly upward, hand on breast, *"como una novela."*

Shit, it was *my* life that was like a novela. Night after night waking up in a dark room to voices shouting and screaming. My father hitting out, my mother poking and probing with her sharp words, her sharp tongue, like a picador with a bull—getting back at him by enraging him some more. My father's heavy hand, heavy feet. My sister rushing in like a terrier, yapping, yapping, sticking herself in the middle, butting my father, pushing the temperature up, upping the ante, raising the stakes. And me—I stand still, I stand there holding myself in, as if I could still my mother's tongue by going mute, as if I could stay my father's hand by standing paralyzed, as if I could cool them all down by freezing myself to death. As if I could cool them all down by freezing myself to death!

Funny I didn't turn out one of those cardboard-faced even-toned no feeling prudes, ain't it? Funny I didn't freeze.

Just the contrary. Heck, I think I was jealous. I had no room in that family, no scope for my talents. But the minute I left home and moved in with Jacob. . . pow! I was my mother in a novela, my father in a fit, my sister in her sneer!

Poor Jacob. I'd picked him out because he was not like any of them. No temperament, no demands. Quiet, gentle, loving—sweet, really, a sweet guy. God knows why he picked me. Maybe he saw the potential for a bit of T.N.T. and matches in his damped-down emotional life. I sure hope so. Cause he sure got some.

I mean, here I spend twenty years of my life with three escapees from a bad melodrama, I go in search of sanity and love in a mad world, I find it. And then what do I go and do? I re-form the repertory company and put on my own show.

Really, I was shocked and ashamed. I was pretty naive at nineteen, well, all through my twenties. Naive as all shit. I thought all I had to do to change the way my life had been was to SAY. Say things like, "I'm not going to live in a tragicomedy any more." Or, "I'm never going to hit *my* children." Or, "I'm not going to be scared and in pain when I give birth." Oh dear. It's sad, really. Somebody should've told me. Not that I'd've listened. The kind of people that told me it was harder than all that were the same folks who told me not to try and change anything, ever. "Go fight City Hall." That's what my neighbor, Olga, used to say about most anything. That was what most of everybody I knew, met, and grew up with used to think: "Go fight

City Hall." And in New York City, City Hall was the Rock of Gibraltar, Mount Everest, and the Atlantic Ocean all rolled into one. Immovable. Go fight City Hall.

Well, I showed them! The next thing I did was take on City Hall, Washington, D.C., the CIA, the FBI and the City's Finest, all in one go. I joined the Communist Party!

No, that doesn't come across right. Not enough shock value. Not here, not now, in 1982. No. I've gotta set the stage first.

O.K. It's 1949, see? World War II ended four years ago. Truman had dropped a couple of A-bombs on two Japanese cities in 1945. He announced the cold war in 1946. The Unamerican Activities Committee started the McCarthy era in 1947. Congress passed anti-red laws with jail sentences for anyone just *thinking* about wanting to overthrow the U.S. Government in 1948 or '49 or so. They revamped the old concentration camps that held the Japanese during the war and thought of building a couple more in nice desolate dry places of the country for when they rounded up the reds and pinks and rose-colored. The leaders of the C.P. were on trial or in hiding, the members were tearing up their membership cards every day! *Women's Day* ran stories about Russian invasions of the U.S. and Russian teachers taking over our schools and closing our children's wide-open little minds. People were being pursued in the streets, hounded out of their jobs, denounced by their neighbors. And what does Conchita's little girl go and do, esa niña loca? What does Ramoncito's little girl go and do? She becomes a red, joins the Communist Party, takes on city hall.

How's that for chutzpah? How's that for up yours, baby, for what the books I read call *épatez les bourgeois*. If that didn't epatez them, I don't see what would have. Living in sin only got a tsk-tsk out of 'em.

But it wasn't all like that. Cause some part of me just went all sort of comfy and at home being in that embattled minority. Some part of me is never comfortable unless I'm doing that kind of uncomfortable thing. I think it's the part of me that stood still as a statue when my family fought, the part of me that swore I'd never hit my children, that cries over all the massacres in the history books, all the deaths behind the anthropology textbooks, or in the newspaper and on the radio. The hatred of pain and injustice of that brown-eyed skinny puertorican girl gets stirred up, and then. . . bang! There I am, in the front lines again.

There's nothing I want more than that, than the end to so much unnecessary pain. I wanted it then, I want it now, and I'll die wanting it. I wish I could die having it, but that doesn't look too likely.

You know, it's hard for me to take the end of the world seriously. I guess cause I grew up *here* and in the thirties, not in Europe where people were getting fed to ovens or in Asia where hundreds of thousands got incinerated at one go, but here where you could hear about it but not experience it, where you could think it could all be stopped. But I take the end of that kind of horror real serious. I go and work it the way I set out to sew a quilt, snip by snip, stitch by stitch, a lot of boring repetitious labor but with the vision of the end product clear in my mind: glorious pattern and color and warmth and comfort. Glorious comfort to last many, many lifetimes.

That's what being a communist, a socialist has meant to me, being a feminist, a radical, a so-called troublemaker. And if I could epatez a few bourgeois while I was at it, so much the better.

Well, I seem to have changed the subject pretty effectively. I was stuck on showing you how I went from a good, quiet, well-behaved girl to a stormy, bad-tempered young woman who wasn't expecting the new role. And how dramatizing a lot is like making up a story, sort of. That reminds me that there was a time when I did some real acting. I mean, regular plays, on-stage kind of acting. High school. I was part of the drama club and the radio club. I remember in the radio club there was an all-woman production, and I had most of the parts. Well, face it, I was the only one with a deep voice; everyone else sounded like a kid or a bird, all high and chirpy. My voice is low and mellow and on the air sounded just lovely. I liked that a lot, of course.

But I used to hate my voice when I was little. The teacher didn't even have to lift her head to look to know it was me talking. "Zorei-da!" she'd say, "Zoe-reh-dar! Stop talking!" Ugh. I used to hate my name, too. I stood out so, was so different. "Oooh," grownups would say in their fakey-fake make-believe-interested voices, "oooh what an *IN-teresting* name! Where are you from, little girl?" From right here, you bitch! No, that wasn't what I really said. I was a good little girl, remember. I'd say "Puerto Rico" and watch the oh-oh sort of look creep up over their faces before they tightened up their *how-nice* look. It still happens, you know. All sorts of people you kinda hoped wouldn't turn out like that. They get a kind of flat look in their eyes, not the interested, excited look they'd get if I said "Spain" or "Argentina" or something else exotic and faraway and not associated in their ratty little minds with cockroaches or welfare or knives.

There was a whole big part of my life, my teens mostly, when I wanted to forget I was puertorican. I used to look in the mirror front-face and try to look like Hedy Lamarr cause if I looked side-face, I could see my oh-so-foreign cheekbones and shaped head. I tried to feel 100 percent American which of course meant white and an-glo, not Indian—red Indian, you know, the real 100 percenters. But there was my name. No getting away from it. Zoreida Alvarez, right at the front of the alphabet so it'd get called right off and everyone would turn and look at me. Zohrehdar Elvrez. Pretty ugly-sounding said that way. Jeez, no wonder I hated it.

It was years before I really got to like it and I guess to like myself too. Jacob helped. He really dug Puerto Rico and puertoricans and plátanos and arroz con pollo and learned some Spanish words off my father first thing. It sure helped to get my family over getting pissed that I'd moved in with him. I mean, it was Jacob I was living in sin with, not some títere off the streets, that nice Jewish boy who loved fried eggs con plátanos maduros fritos y aguacate and knew how to say sinvergüenza and canalla and coño and all sorts of other puertorican insults and bad words. My father especially. It reconciled him—I think that's the word. My mother didn't need much reconciling. She'd handed me over to a GOOD MAN, not one of her villains, a man who wouldn't beat me, abuse me, kill me. The man in the white hat on the white horse, that one. And when she got into the horror of her existence in a low, husky, full-of-suffering voice, she would pause, raise her eyes to heaven and look thankful to God and the Virgin Mary and half-a-dozen saints and say, "Gracias a Dios, mi hijita tiene un hombre bueno que la cuide." And then down with the eyes, back to the tale of woe.

Take care of me? Stuff! I did the taking care of. Trust nobody to see that though. That kind of thing is real invisible, especially in the fifties. That kid of work wasn't even *there*, except just you stop doing it and boy, you'd get noticed all right. Not just shopping and cooking and dishwashing and laundry and beds and floors and bathrooms, but feelings and you know. . . mothering. No wonder I had scope for temperament. I had a shitload of work I hadn't counted on especially as we'd contracted to a free union, an *arrangement* between equals. We didn't get married to avoid all that artificial stuff and the herr-leader complex for the guy, and the sweet-little-woman stuff for me. We were young communists and enlightened and knew about male chauvinism and the household slavery of women and Engels on the family. But I came away with 90 percent of the housework and 95 percent of the emotional mending and ironing any old how.

But I was telling you about acting when I got into all this, about how I was in plays in high school and college. It's strange really. I was so shy it was painful. Not just for me, I'm sure. You've seen people like that, so shy it's painful to watch. But from real little I liked being on stage. I was the carrot in the grade school play on good nutrition and remember reciting a piece about Cordell Hull for assembly, except what I remember was not raising my voice or his picture high enough. Learned my lesson. I can project with the best of them now.

In high school I did some scenes from Shakespeare. *As You Like It*, I think it was. I was fair Rosalind in a long dress and my rhinestones being diamonds around my neck and a well-born high haughty posture to my head. Yum. That was fun. In college we did a play about nuns and I wanted the lead so bad it hurt, but I missed out and became the old nun instead. I did men's parts a lot, you better believe it, with my voice in an all-girls school. I liked hitching up my pants legs when I sat. Standing masculinelike, thrusting my hips forward, hands in my pockets.

But I was still shy and it cost me a lot to get up there on the first night with a whole lot of people in front. I usually was sick that night or right after. I'd catch bad colds or get the runs. It's strange really.

Of course, now I know better. It makes a kind of sense: I know I needed to make people notice me, and if you're shy and a good girl to boot, it's hard to get any attention in real life. Getting up on stage, though, and getting your lines handed to you and with someone there to direct and correct you—"No, stand a little further forward. Look at him as if he were a worm. That's right." See, that was easier! And attention by the barrel load.

When I left school and moved in with Jacob and became a communist I had other things to do and I didn't act any more, not for years and years and years. Of course I had the attention of the FBI, the Puerto Rican Secret Service, the cops, and all sorts of vigilant anti-red citizens. But that's not the same. And of course I got to enact dramatic scenes over a scorched pot or a broken teapot, but that's not the same. No, I missed the stage. There's a kind of clean feeling about proper acting, a clean good feeling when you do it right and what you get is applause and admiration, not suspicion, not jail sentences, not anger and sulks which is what I got, mostly, for being a red or bad-tempered. No. I missed that. Didn't know I missed it, but I did.

When I look back, you know, all that reading I did for the children? That was acting. I didn't tell them stories, but I read them other people's stories, acted them out. I loved it, kept it up till they were quite grown up and I was reading them proper novels. I had a ball. That's what I miss about their growing up and going away. One thing anyway. Yeah.

But I'm glad they're launched and out there and O.K. I guess I'm glad *I'm* here and launched and O.K., too! Cause I am, you know. I am.

The Flute

*In a time of self-doubt I ask myself to have a dream.
I cry out, torn between conflicting pressures: What
is my life for? Then I lie down to sleep. I dream.*

I am a medicine man among a people who live in the southwest, in
a land of red earth. I am old. There is need among my people for
me to have a dream, so we create a sacred circle for me to dream
in. A white circle is painted on the red clay, and I lie within it, on
my side, in a position called running dog, so I can travel far in the
dream countries.

Almost at once I become a dog, and I find myself running through
a green forest. I hear a voice telling me that I must follow Grey Fox
no matter where it goes. That I must instantly do whatever it does,
without hesitation, or I will be lost. Also, I must watch out for the
tricks of False Dog, who will try to distract me by getting me to follow him instead. I see Grey Fox ahead and keep running. Fox ducks
into a hollow log, and I follow. I shoot out the other end into the
sunlight and see a grey shape ahead of me in the woods, but I realize at once it is False Dog. I remember in the middle of the log there
was a hole going down, with sunlight shining through it. I double
back into the log and throw myself into the hole.

I fall out into the sky of another world. It is a wide plain with red
mesas bordering it. As I fall, I see Grey Fox running across the plain
toward some high red cliffs, and as soon as I land, I run after it. We
run as fast as the wind across the plain, and I am panting heavily,
trying to keep up with Fox. It runs up a path in the side of the cliff
and into the mouth of a cave, and I run after it.

As soon as I enter the cave I stop. There is a fire burning in one
end of the cave and a tunnel going off to the other side. There are
large red figures tending the fire, and I know they are clay people

and that this is the cave of the Sacred Winds and they are the keepers of the Winds. But which way has Fox gone? I start to run down the tunnel, but the figure running ahead turns to look over its shoulder and I see the red eyes of the False Dog. I double back and run into the bay of rock where the fire is, just in time to see Grey Fox jump into the fire. I know I must not hesitate, so I jump in after it. In the fire, our bodies are burnt completely away, except for one long bone each. The firetenders take us out and turn us into flutes.

Then they take us to the mouth of the cave. We look out and see everything has changed. We are high above the earth now. There are clouds below us, and far, far below, a green plain where two groups of people are gathered. They are praying and calling out and crying up to the keepers in the cave, asking to be sent poets, medicine ones, singers of the great Song. The keepers throw us out of the cave, and as we fall through the mist we gather new bodies around us. The mouthpiece and six holes of the flutes become the chakras of our bodies. When we land, we are people. I am myself, and Grey Fox has become Bernice Reagon. She and her people go off in one direction, and my people carry me off in another. They are pleased with the gifts they have received and give thanks that their prayers have been answered.

And . . .

*This dream came to me in the fall of 1983, in the
months after a serious head injury, as I was strug-
gling to return to the full use of language and of
my whole mind.*

There was a group of people who were both Asian and Latin, like
Filipinos. They were very beautiful, with smooth brown skin, black
hair, and straight, even white teeth. This tribe were all poets. This
is what they did as a people, and they were famous for it. One young
woman had been struck on the head and lay in a coma. Her father,
brother, and another male relative, perhaps a cousin or her lover, wrote
a letter to the government protesting what had been done to her.
The following night they were all found dead, each of the men who
had signed the letter. It was clear that a death squad had retaliated
against them for speaking up.

Now the only poet left in the family was a young girl or boy, an an-
drogynous being who was just about to receive initiation to become
a full poet. This young person was standing before the old woman
who was the teacher for the poets of the tribe, the one who taught
them their craft and passed on the wisdom. She had a great big heavy
book in which everything a poet needed to know, including everything that had happened to them, was written. She was showing the
young poet her book. The events of the massacre had already been
written into the book, and now a new chapter was beginning. It was
about what to do after a traumatic, horrible event in our lives. The
first page had a quote on it from Oscar Wilde. It said:

> When struck in the mouth by the hand's edge
> or the iron bar, the poet always has one word
> (or one weapon) left in his arsenal: *AND.*

In the dream, this meant that whatever happened, one could always start again from that point. As long as there was life, the poet could begin again just by saying "AND." They would silence her and she would say *AND* and they would be defeated.

Then I saw a picture of some embroidery that stopped abruptly. It was as if there had been an earthquake and there was now a fault line, a slippage in the fabric, and the embroidery couldn't begin again at the same place, but only several inches lower. Looking at it I understood that I shouldn't struggle to get back to where I was before the accident. Instead, I should begin again, from where I now was, by saying *AND*.

In My Grandmother's House

My grandmother turns eighty the day I arrive. The next day at lunch, she says out of nowhere, "Do not go gentle into that good night, rage, rage against the dying of the light, you know?" and looks at me, the family poet. "But what can you do?" she asks. I don't know what to say to her at this stage of the game. Most of the time she talks in long, complaining monologues, asking the universe (since she doesn't believe in God), why Dick doesn't write, why Jeff isn't happier in school, why Greg isn't happier period, why no one became a surgeon, why Dick and Ben don't get along, why she has no great-grandchildren yet, why she never got to live in Manhattan the way she always wanted to, why the others don't help take care of her sister who has had a stroke, why everything has gone wrong.

I am working on a book. I have a publisher lined up. I tell her about it, knowing the pleasure she takes in such visible achievements. My grandmother says musingly, "I never understood why you didn't go into commercial television." I stare at her, dumbfounded. "Why on earth would I want to?" She says, "It's very creative." If I won the Pulitzer she'd want to know why it wasn't the Nobel. If I got the Nobel, she'd want me to have two. When I was a child she wanted me to be Miss Puerto Rico in the Puerto Rico Day Parade, and she wanted Prince Charles to see me and fall in love with me: the first Puerto Rican Jewish Queen of England!

I get her to open once again the box of old photographs, to tell me who is who: my cousin B, her children, my mother's cousins. . .they died in the war. . .and this is my mother when she was eighteen, before she married my father. . .oh look here I am in my first fancy dress. . .she laughs with pleasure, clapping her hands. Look at that lace. . .I felt so grown up! This is Rube. . .isn't he handsome? What is the first thing you remember? I ask her. Do you remember Russia? No she says. I remember only the boat. I remember we were all on the deck together. *The sun was shining. The place we slept was smelly, stuffy, dark and crowded, so all the people were out on the deck as much as possible, sharing food, talking, laughing, playing music. Some of the other passengers were playing accordions and fiddles and I began to dance in the middle of the deck. I danced and danced and all the people around me were laughing and clapping and watching me as I spun round and round in my short skirts. It was the happiest moment of my life.*

She tells me about some book my father read that she claims got him interested in genetics. "If only he hadn't read that book," she sighs, "he might have been a doctor, and we might have a cure for cancer in the family." Her other son *is* a doctor, but he hasn't found the cure either. I wonder what hopes she had for him. She is at the end of her life, and looking back, she is dissatisfied. She tells me she wanted to be a lawyer, "but Rube said women had to be too aggressive to make it as lawyers. He was afraid I would become hard." So she became a legal secretary instead, and later worked for a publishing house. She says she wanted to be a writer as well. "But I have no talent," she sighs, sorrowfully. She asks, for the hundredth time, why it is that the guts in the family skipped a generation. "My mother was so courageous," she sighs, "and my sons!" The genetics of courage, skipping generations.

I try to tell her what I think. I say things were hard, the anti-Semitism, the red-baiting, then the Holocaust wiping out all trace of that village in the Ukraine where she was born, and most of her extended family of cousins and neighbors. Everything driving her toward conformity, safety, security. She tells me, without batting an eye, that she has never experienced anti-Semitism because she lived only with Jews, all her life.

Changing the subject, I tell her we are going out to see *Yentl* at the local Brighton Beach theater. She says, "You know, Barbra Streisand has a terrible nose. Somehow they do something with the cameras so it doesn't show so much, but she has a terrible nose." I say, "Whaddya mean *terrible*? She has a big, beautiful nose. She's gorgeous, that woman!" "A terrible, terrible nose," my grandmother sighs, shaking her head.

Looking at a photograph of my father's family, all gathered around a table for some Thanksgiving dinner when I was three or four or five, what I see is the stiffness of their faces, the undercurrents of terror. Only Mom and Pop, the immigrants, look openly wary, but it seems to me the smiles and laughter on all the other faces hide jitters, nervousness, a shying away from the camera's eye, or frantic storytelling to hide the pit below. Everything is fine, fine, just fine. This terror of Jews is like the terror of incest: a childhood in which brothers, fathers, uncles, grandfathers can turn into monsters has no safety in it anywhere. A world in which the village can become one huge trench filled with bodies and then be bulldozed over, where the shtetl is set on fire by the men who yesterday bought your milk or timber or hay, had you make their daughter's wedding dress, sold you a goat, borrowed to buy a new plow, has no safety in it anywhere.

So they keep their eyes fixed straight ahead, not looking into the shadowy corners. Not to see unpleasantness. To avoid strong emotions. Not to make a fuss over little pains. To keep as low a profile as possible, but at the same time pushing to have brilliant, indispensable sons. (And attractive, popular daughters, well-married to other brilliant sons.) My cousins were brought up to read, but not too much; to think, but not too much; encouraged to obsess about boyfriends and fix their hair, to be more like the women of this new country were supposed to be. A change from the pride of the previous generations in their literacy and multilinguality, my great-aunt Mae saying from her stroke survivor's bed, "I always read the papers cover to cover. Freiheit, People's World, The Guardian." It was the war and the fifties that did them in, this community of boisterous, Yiddish-speaking, theater-going, May Day-marching rebels and radicals, going limp and self-protective with fear. This is the undertow to the picture of a happily celebrating family of successful generations, up from the shtetl. That the monster, the enemy, the expulsion, the sirens, the soldiers will surely, inevitably come someday.

So my grandmother collects famous people she has met on boats or knows the relatives of, collects connections like her grandson's college romance with the grand-niece of the Pope. (I see her press-

ing her face to the wire of the new camp fences, saying, 'but we are intimately connected with his Holiness the Pope!') Collects the achievements of her offspring like guarantees against bad luck, insurance against the worst, and still nothing is enough for her, nothing can guarantee anything, not one person's safety is assured. It is out of her love for us that she picks and complains about the very achievements she demands of us, wanting more, always more.

Passing: the pretense that we're O.K., that everything's fine, that the guarantees work. Pretending to believe we are not in any danger from the things that our ancestors fled, the things our kin in other countries, in other political moments are endangered by.

Pretense, because my mother told me this: If she learned nothing else from living among Jews at the time of the Holocaust (and she did learn much, much more), it was that passing does not work, that the successful, professional, well-connected Jews were also taken away, in the same trains with the rest, that it didn't work, that whole carefully constructed net of supposed guarantees. That she would always be Puerto Rican no matter who she married and how she spoke. They could find her. And still, she married whiter and wealthier, and still she speaks with a clipped Britishified tongue, does it anyway, in search of safety.

And someone said to me (it was amazing when she said it, like a dawn in my mind showing me the lay of the land), that Israel itself, as a country, is trying to pass, is pretending that weapons and industry and armies will be the guarantees, that it's a safe country like other countries, that surely it can't happen now. And like my grandmother reaching for some achievement that will be enough, nothing quite makes the grade, brings satisfaction, heals the terror.

Our last night in Brooklyn we all go out to dinner. When my grandmother wants dessert, she tries to talk us into ordering it, but she won't get one for herself. We urge her again and again but she says, "No, no, you get one for you." We finally agree to get one incredibly frilled and ruffled french pastry and share it among us. We'll all taste it, we say. We set it in front of her. She keeps passing it around, eyeing it greedily every step of the way, her mouth obviously watering for it. She presses it on my brother. He pretends to take a bite and passes it back. In this way we coax her into feeding herself some sweetness. I find it hard to breathe. I am filled with horror at her self-denial, at the way she holds tightly to her dissatisfactions, complaining about what she hasn't got, afraid to reach out for what she wants.

I will probably never know exactly how she was terrified out of daring, what the rewards and punishments were, the turning points, the seeming points of no return. In her presence I am angry both at her and for her. In her presence I want to shake her out of worrying forever. To say, "Then do *not* go gentle, dammit, make a scene!" When I am away, I continue to write letters in answer to her reproachful notes, mourning, not the approaching death of her body, but the other ones: all the little deaths and disappointments of her spirit that began long, long ago. Sometime after she danced and spun to the music of accordions on the deck of the S.S. Bremmen, in the sun and wind.

Bailando Sola

to mami

Sola   tan tán, tiquitán
tan sola   tan tán, tiquitán
tan sola   tan tán, tiquitán tan tán

Her hand on her stomach
The other in the air
Feet go
Hips go

   ¡Baila!   tan tán, tiquitán tan
   ¡Baila!   tan tán, tiquitán tan
   ¡Baila!   tan tán, tiquitán tan tán

Maracas on the radio
Guitarras, drums
Y nadie, mamita
(just me in the corner)
nadie, mamita, te
   mira,   tan tán, tiquitán tan
   mira,   tan tán, tiquitán tan
   ¡Mira! tan tán, tiquitán tan tán

Watching your body
Watching your face
You tilt your head
You close your eyes
Oh, is she crying?
No! see, she smiles
   dancing!   tan tán, tiquitán tan
   dancing!   tan tán, tiquitán tan
   dancing!   tan tán, tiquitán tan tán

I watch in the mirror
I practice the steps
I learn how to dance it
to live it
to live it
to live and live through it
    sola   tan tán, tiquitán
    tan sola   tan tán, tiquitán
    tan sola   tan tán, tiquitán
               tan tán, tiquitán
               tan tán, tiquitán tan tán

Old

Una

My mother at thirty was as luminous as a Puerto Rican dawn over the cream sand beaches curving in and out and around the island. She was like the moist fruit of the mango, like the fronds of the royal palm in the wind. And I knew thirty was what I was going to be when I lost the skeleton I wore, when I grew old, grew beautiful and free.

Dos

Skin
practicing to be old—
lining up,
squaring off:
tracings
etchings
bas relief.

Look!
Over the blue
creek beds of my veins,
how the wrinkling
ripples sparkle
in the sun.

Tres

Que clase de vieja will I be when I knew none, grew up in New York City when El Barrio was young like me and grandmothers grew in Puerto Rico, when grandmothers were kept fresh in boxes of pictures under the bed and became flesh only the summer I was going to be ten. We took a long sickening boat ride of a week to the magical landscape of Naranjito and on its one street I became "¡Mira! la hija de Lola, la de Mercedes." Abuela Mercedes was just like her photograph: large, cotton-wrapped, her breasts squared off onto her middle, hammocks of face dripping onto her chin, cushions of her melting into the brown floorboards. She smelled like maduros frying. And while the music from the jukebox across the street flies about her shoulders, crashes into the hibiscus bush, the guayaba, and as she stands imperturbable, solid, only her flesh giving way, I am comforted and afraid.

I cannot turn to my other grandmother. Abuela Rosario sat small, sat thin, sat straight and hard in a hard chair, knobbed hands on a knobbed stick. She beat one girl and ten boys into adulthood, and my father beat me, and I beat my babies and bit my hands and looked for knobs.

Cuatro

Crow's wings not feet—pinions
anchored to my eyes.
They spread in flight only
when I smile.
I smile.

Cinco

She warned me as she added sugar to the roasting coffee beans to blacken the brew, "Don't go out into the damp air, the cool night, after a day tostando café in an open pan over a hot fire, porque te va' a pa'mar." She said, "¡Cuidao, o te va' a pa'mar!" And she meant that the moment I hit the evening chill my warm skin would shrivel and wrinkle and ruck, a surrealer Rip Van Winkle. Only a moment would go by and I'd be old, old, older than old doña Cornelia herself, who always carefully wrapped a towel around her head and shoulders like a shawl before she left her burnt-sugar brown kitchen and stepped out beneath the banana leaves hiding the stars.

Seis

Maga was Jane's mother, my best friend's mother, was Alabama-born, high-born, white as her hair, and even after twenty years in Puerto Rico couldn't speak Spanish, and her a communist like her red-haired daughter, like her Puerto Rican son-in-law, like me.

I wanted to be like her when I grew old, I wanted the freedom to say what I liked, when I liked, to whom I liked. I wanted to pour Lapsang Souchong out of a china teapot into the endless afternoon and tell others what to do and how to do it. I wanted what I thought it felt like, sitting tall and high-handed, hair cut short and crisp, straight spine keeping the cops from stepping through the door to take her son-in-law César away, lean slacks bending, lean hands reaching to grasp the garden weeds and smack the roots free of soil, grasping, too, at her daughter's home, her son, her time and when Jane died, she reached for mine.

I couldn't give you that! But oh, Maga, will I sit as you sat, lonehanded, sipping tepid tea into the night?

Siete

Stop!
I don't want my scalp
    shining through a few thin hairs.
Don't want my neck skin to hang—
    neglected cobweb—in the corner of my chin.

Stop! at ruckling ruches of skin
    at soft sags,
        bags of tongue tickling breast and belly,
    at my carved face.

No further.
Stop.

Ocho

no quiero morir

California

I.

In the middle of writing about the grimness of Chicago, about my disorientation as a newly arrived immigrant of thirteen, I look out the window and notice I am in California. That I've been here ten years, longer than I've lived in any one place before. I remember how strange the Spanish architecture on Chabot Street looked the day I arrived, and all the gardens full of succulents. How thrown I was by the odd mixture of vegetation from places I've loved—pine and hibiscus, bougainvillea and maple, and all sorts of strange Martian-looking, green defomities with delicate fringed and puffed blossoms poking out at odd angles. And the whiteness of the light. Eastern sunlight had been yellow, deciduous, moist. Here it was leafless and white and dry. Intense enough to imprint itself not only on my retina, but on the insides of my lungs. This is the place no one took me or sent me to. The place I chose for myself.

Place. How I always begin with place: the most potent imagery for a wandering Jew, an immigrant Puerto Rican. "What will this place give me, do to me? What landscapes, what houses will it leave in my dreams? What layers will it add to the collage of my identity, my skin, my permanent passport?"

Ten years later I am in California and it's summer. Soft air and warm breezes and fragrance on the streets. A whiff of honey this morning as I pass a tree with minute bunches of white hairs arranged in bouquets between dark green leaves. The showering down of Japanese incense from a plum tree in full pink blossom hiding the black branches from sight.

2.

I have filled a beautiful blue and turquoise cup with orange and golden nasturtiums with their peculiar musty scent of dank earth. The scent that surrounds old tin bathtubs set outside in the sun of twenty years ago on the cement in front of our house on the mountaintop in Puerto Rico. The water would sparkle in the sun while I splashed in the tub, and the air was hot and thick with the smells of flowering nasturtiums and cherry tomatoes heavy with small orange fruit, and all around me the hibiscus bushes rustled with lizards and reinitas, and the lichen-stained cement of the cistern was criss-crossed with the scurrying of ants.

As I wrote those words, a truck pulled up to this house and delivered two five-gallon bottles of spring water, sweet to quench thirst on hot California days. Water that doesn't need to be boiled or have the ten drops of bleach measured into it: poison just sufficient to kill the bacteria from the dead lizards and frogs that decayed in our water tank.

Today I notice I'm in California and I have survived the bacteria in the tank and the invasions of McCarthy and the FBI, survived the anger of my mother and the passivity of my father, survived the loneliness I thought I would die of, and the violence and fear and violations of my growing up. I have become taller than the nasturtiums, able to breathe above them. Now I walk through them, picking and choosing, parting the flat floppy leaves to find the blooms I want, arranging them in this ceramic cup made by a Mendocino potter and glazed the color of the tropical sea at noon. The flowers I cull from the gardens of my mothers and fathers, but the cup is completely mine, and I have set the whole and glowing combination here on my desk to dazzle the eye.

3.

This is the life I chose before I was born, when the twin creature who floated beside me died and was reabsorbed into the pink walls of our world, and I decided to go on. The life I chose during the long, choking hours of labor before my first breath.

The life I chose the first time I picked up a pencil and saw that the page was absolutely mine, and as big as the world.

The life I chose when I promised my six-year-old self never to forget being a child, never to grow frightened and dishonest like the grownups I saw, nodding politely to each other without affection, and decided to put my true self in a time capsule for later use.

The life I chose when I filled notebook after notebook and promised to remember everything of importance.

The life I chose when I did not die of loneliness but fed myself crumbs I carefully gathered: six eggrolls worth of self-love, all at a sitting, and the deep golden cups of cheap tea, endlessly replenished for free.

4.

There is a picture before me of my great-grandparents standing in dark coats, black and grey, on the boardwalk in Brooklyn, in an older, colder immigrant community. I am an immigrant too, I tell them. Twice, thrice the immigrant. I was torn from the moist soil of Indiera, roots ripping, and transplanted to stony ground. I have dug myself carefully up and planted myself here. You would be proud of me, Leah. I have finally learned to make gardens.

There was a table with an umbrella over it on my great-grandmother's porch, always set with a bowl full of fruit, and we would sit there on long, warm afternoons. I remember Leah coming out from the shadows of the doorway into the blazing light of the porch in summer with a plate of knishes fresh from the oven: potato, cabbage, spinach, lemon, onion, kasha. For years I mourned the fact that she died without teaching me to make them, the secrets of dough and filling gone. But looking around me, I see that I know what I need to know: I have come into rooms with the same movements, carrying plates of tostones, crisp golden and garlicky, I have remembered her standing in sunshine, and I have begun to tell her story and mine.

5.

On my birthday I dream of a tablecloth, white and yellow in a large plaid, the corner lifting in a light breeze, flapping gently. On the table is your bowl, Leah, filled with the cool fruit of the temperate zone, plums and green grapes and nectarines and fuzzy peaches with red hearts. My table now. The table of the choosers of life.

If I Forget Thee, Oh Jerusalem

If I Forget Thee, Oh Jerusalem

All through that summer and fall of the Israeli invasion of Lebanon and the massacres in Beirut, I felt an urgent need to write about what was happening, but no words would come, the conflicting emotions immobilizing my hand and tongue. Sometime during those months of rage and silence, a phrase began to ring in me like a bell: *If I forget thee, oh Jerusalem.* It ran through my mind like a bright thread as I carried water along a mountain path in Puerto Rico and fell into the rhythm of my steps as I walked in the Vermont woods with my parents. I would hear it, faint and shining, as I drifted off to sleep in the cold November nights of Minnesota and as I made my way back toward California, I began to write it on scraps of paper, in the margins of my journal, and finally the words began to come. And so one night I called up the Berkeley Public Library and asked them to look up the reference for me. The woman came back after a few minutes and told me the line came from Psalm 137. I hung up and quickly turned to the right page in the Gideon Bible I stole from a motel room in Wyoming. As I read, I felt shivers go up my spine. In the three sections of the ancient poem were the three pieces of what I wanted to say. This was what had been ringing deep in me: a buried song.

The first verse spoke of the bitterness of slavery and exile, the grief of captivity and loss. The second was a vow to remember freedom, to keep it as a bright vision, an inheritance, to know ourselves as free people, however heavy the terms of our bondage. The third was a cry for vengeance at whatever cost, a pledge to return all our pain with interest and let it fall like a curse even if it were on the heads of children not yet born. As I read the words aloud to myself over and over, I understood what it was that I had to say. I sat down and began to write.

Psalm 137

By the rivers of Babylon
there we sat down
and we wept
as we remembered Zion.
We hung our harps on the willows
and hid them in the midst thereof,
for those that carried us away into captivity
required of us a song
and they that wasted us required of us mirth, saying
"Sing us one of the songs of Zion,"
but how shall we sing Thy song
in a strange land?

If I forget thee, oh Jerusalem,
let my right hand forget its uses.
If I do not remember thee
let my tongue cleave to the roof of my mouth
if I prefer not Jerusalem above my chief joy.

Remember, dear God, these children of Edom, in the days
of Jerusalem
who cried raze it, raze it, even to the foundations.
Oh, you daughter of Babylon
who wilt in time be destroyed,
happy shall they be that reward thee
as thou hast served us.
Happy shall they be
that taketh and dasheth thy little ones
against the stones.

I.

I am traveling when the news begins. At night, surrounded by the sounds of the tropics, I learn what has happened during the day. With each wave of invasion, each map with arrows on the evening news, it becomes harder to speak, a logjam of emotions blocking my words, and beneath, an icy river of fear. One evening I sit in front of the TV on a mountaintop in Puerto Rico, watching the fuzzy satellite pictures of the PLO leaving Beirut, the start of another long, bitter exile, and feel the tears rise in me. "Oh, my people," I whisper, meaning those taut young faces, those hands gripping the edges of the trucks that file past the camera, gripping their rifles held high into the air, a Palestinian flag snapping in the wind. . .and the faces of those left behind, watching their beloved hope, their protection, moving away in the dusty light. Meaning the Jews, those being drilled in the desert to carry out acts like these, those sitting at home like me, watching the evening news with a knot of grief and terror in their throats.

Seeing my face, Ginín asks, "¿Dónde queda eso? ¿Quiénes son? ¿Cuáless son los malos?" Where is that place? Who are those people? Who are the bad guys? Rogelio shouts from across the room, "The ones in the trucks are terrorists, the americanos are on the other side and just kicked the asses of these fellows. It's over in . . .¿Cómo se llama eso? What's that place?" Their geography is immediate, tangible: the shape of Las Torres or Sierra Gularte against the sky, the net of paths running through these mountains, the exact contour of each hill, each plot of land they work. Beyond the borders of their daily work there is "the north." Other places they know no more of than that newscaster knows of East Oakland or this coffee farm. "Se llama Palestina," I say. "Those people are farmers. Their land is being taken away. The ones in the trucks were fighting back, protecting them. They are fighting over the land, over who can live there." I am shaking with rage that I cannot stop what is being done. That it is being done in the name of protecting Jews. That there are those who will believe that it is in my interest as a Jew, that by being a Jew I have agreed to these acts committed in my name. A logjam of emotions, and beneath, an icy river of fear.

2.

September 20th. Each night since the first news of the massacres we turn on the radio at dinnertime to hear the Canadian broadcast. We've all had trouble digesting our food. Tonight the broadcaster's voice says, "400,000 Israelis demonstrated today against the massacres in Beirut, demanding Begin's resignation," and I begin to cry, knowing I've been holding my breath for a month. The words come from my mouth without premeditation: Thank God! Thank God, now they can't. . .what? Round us up? Line us up and shoot us for what the generals have done? Consider us guilty, all of us, of standing by in complicit silence? Now Jews have marched. Four hundred thousand Israelis have separated themselves from the crime.

3.

It seems unspeakable that in the face of Sabra and Chatila the fear in my heart is for myself, for us, for Jews. Now that there is loud, visible outrage in Israel, I can breathe again, and feel pain, and the pain I feel is the weight of Jewish history lived out in my nightmares of Cossacks and camps and trains, of smoke rising against the sky, in my daily shrinking from the expected blow.

But how could Jews do this?

I hear the question over and over again. And why should we be better than other people? I have learned that suffering does not improve people, that slavery does not ennoble us for freedom, that oppression springs from oppression, echoing the twisted lessons we learn from our pain. Don't tell me otherwise. I have watched Israeli soldiers recreating the piles of bodies, the mass graves, the camps filled with death, the heaps of rubble, practicing the lesson, "Those who win are the ruthless. No one will protect us, so we must protect only ourselves. Where did compassion for strangers ever get us? WE HAVE NO ALLIES." And my heart answers back, in fear, in grief: It's true, they were too few, too late.

4.

Today a demonstration calling for Begin's resignation was bombed by right-wing Jews. Forgive me, my brother who died there, but my reaction was relief: Now the war is also between Jews. Now it is clearly about the choices we make, not the people we are born into. This is the first time since 1948, says the radio announcer, that Jews have killed Jews over politics in Israel, and so terrible has the other way been that I find myself preferring it this way.

5.

I am not an "exceptional Jew," a "different Jew." Over and over I find myself bringing out the list of good deeds, of righteously radical ancestors, the dates and places of our acts of solidarity: a pedigree, a license, a paper to say we did not sacrifice the Christian son of your great-great-grandparents, we did not charge you 50 percent interest, we never stole your land, cheated you in a sale of jewelry or conspired to take over your country club or your country. We are not even secretly rich. We do not own slum property, and we have never been bosses. Please believe me! In six generations we have always fought the tyrants, walked among the liberators, marched and leafletted for other people's freedoms, been internationalists, heart and soul. Not like those other Jews. Not like the grasping, thieving, cheap, oily, greedy, landgrabbing, dishonest, murdering, shuffling, slumlord Jews whose image crouches in the shadow of pulpits, fills the libraries, is whispered of to children, whose shadow falling across us stops us cold in the act of asking for a raise, complaining about a price, makes us notice, with squirming discomfort, the Jewish names of businesses, ignoring the 1001 other businesses in town. Those Jews scapegoated for doing what people do to survive (so that even the gentiles who bargain for pennies are accused of "jewing you down"), those Jews made bigger than life, the tricks and strategies of getting by that in others are called thrift, called ambitious, called prudent, called admiringly "landing on their feet," labeled in us as particular defects of Jewish character.

I repudiate my own denial. Because even if I were not the child, the grandchild, the great-grandchild of communists, bolsheviks, organizers, even if I had never walked a picket line or carried a banner, even if I cared for no one but myself, had lived all my life by cheating and overcharging, I would have the right to live, to rejoice in my existence as a Jewish woman in this world. It is only fear, only lies I have been told, making me bend my head and heart to the anti-Semitism in the world when I say: "But Jews are always defenders of justice, in the right battles for freedom, but Jews helped build the labor movement, but Jews. . ."

6.

And what can I say in the face of this horror perpetrated, directed, paid for by Jews? That I weep at night for my Palestinian people (who dares to tell me they are not my people)? That I pound the pillow and dream of burning villages? That their faces look like kin to me: brown faces, dark eyes, bones like my own wide cheekbones, Puerto Rican, Ukrainian, who can tell? That my land is also occupied? That as a Latin American I know, in the pulsing of history through my own flesh, the feel of conquest: the cooking bowl shattered, the hearth fire trampled, boots marching over our green fields grinding the tender shoots of our living into the mud. Oh, yes, and the decree nailed to the wall, the prisoners led away and never seen again, that I know about conquest? That their enemy is my enemy?

7.

If these are answers, they are not enough. I speak my solidarity from the voice of the Puerto Rican, not daring to say that I know as much of pillage, of conquest as a Jew (my great-grandmother's face at the kitchen table in Brooklyn showing me the games she played on that little Ukrainian farm of her childhood from which she fled, babies in her arms, from the endless pogroms, the armies, the everlasting taking away—of children, of crops, of animals, of freedom, of life).

I have been told those crimes no longer matter, and so I am afraid to say I know you as a Jew.

In my nightmares I still see the crowds with torches dragging us from our homes. *"Jews!"* they yell. *"Filthy Jews!"* And now and then, *"Imperialist, landgrabbing Jews! You slaughter Christian babies, you eat Palestinian children . . . kill them, burn them, clean the land of their presence. The only way to stop them is once and for all!"* I must answer that voice in me, in the world, in my beloveds, Jewish and gentile, before my solidarity will come clean from my burning heart, from love and identification and not this hiding, crouching terror in me, before I can say, *I am a Jew, and I will safeguard your children with my life.*

8.

We were slaves in Egypt, say the words we are taught to remember, and we were exiles in Babylon, never to forget the days of our bondage, the years of weeping, but no one told us there was a choice about how to remember these facts, or that our survival would depend upon that choice. That we could use the memory of pain to sharpen our vision of freedom, to hold tight to that vision, trace with our fear and sorrow a map to show us exactly what total liberation would look like; or surrender the vision for the vengeance, hug to our chests the pain too heavy to let go, count and recount each blow, each bruise, each death and despoiling, reckon up what is due. No room for visions, anchored to that pain, except as a weapon, except as a shield, for vengeance will come and someone with the eyes, the gestures, the name, the history of our sorrow will stray across our path and then it will be our turn: happy shall they be who give tit for tat, who can torture you back; happy, say the words of the Psalm, shall they be who taketh and dasheth thy little ones against the stones.

9.

Oh, but I remember Jerusalem. When I was a little girl growing up in Puerto Rico, a Jew among Catholics, the child of communists during the McCarthy years, proud of belonging to the righteous few, back then when the Left still supported Israel, when my grandmother still sent me heroic stories of Jewish freedom fighters, when our house was still filled with UNESCO pictures of Israeli children dancing, the same dances I learned at summer camp, the same dances my cousins brought back from the kibbutzim and taught me... back then, I had a vision of Zion, territorio libre, blooming out of the shards of war. I imagined poor people, refugees from all over the world, turning the desert into flowering orange groves with nothing but their bare hands and hope. On the kibbutzim they lived collectively, the children growing up proud and straightbacked and free. (I was a child then and believed I would live to see freedom flower the whole world over. I was a child then and thought freedom was a simple thing, to plant and see bloom from night to morning.) I didn't know the orange groves we bought with our nickels hid the scars of burnt out Palestinian villages, erasing the outlines of beloved gardens, covering up the sites of massacres, murders, rapes. That a whole way of life, a whole people were being plowed under, a crop of hatred being planted among the little green trees, bearing the fruit of war.

I knew none of this and so I loved a visionary land in my mind, a place where people of every color and shape walked in the stone streets of Jerusalem at the heart of the world, the City (said *National Geographic*) Sacred to Three Great Religions. The music would be Arabic and Mediterranean and Eastern European and Latin and African and Asian. The sounds of drums and flutes and bells would drift out of the smaller side streets, and oh, the food! Heaps of glowing fruit and the steaming delicacies of every land. In my vision there were brightly colored streamers and pennants hanging from each window and balcony, a little like Old San Juan at Christmas, and everyone went upright and glad and free in heart and limb.

I don't remember exactly when we stopped talking about Israel. Sometime in those years of my childhood a silence fell and it became a word filled with tightness and anxiety and a host of other unnamed and hidden feelings. Most of us, we, the Jewish Left, disengaged ourselves, removed its hand from our shoulder, denied it was related to us, separated ourselves: it isn't ours, we hastened to explain. We're as anti as anyone. And I, who read *Tricontinental* magazine from cover to cover, who read voraciously about the history and upheavals of Guinea-Bissau and Mozambique, the guerrilla movements of Colombia and Laos, read reports on the death of Che in Bolivia on torture and mineral deposits in Brasil, who wanted to know my world whatever it contained, skipped over the articles about the Middle East, saying it was all "too complicated," that I couldn't make sense of it. And gentile friends who could unravel 500-page tomes of economic theory agreed with me that anti-Semitism was just too complex, and I continued to feel that anyone else's pain would be easier.

What I want to ask now is what we did with the vision when the reality proved sordid. What I want to know is how we gave it up. I want to know what we did with the love.

10.

But now it seems to me that Zionism asks too little, not too much! They have traded in that City of the vision for a cramped fortress tower, believing that Jews will always be persecuted, hunted. That most of humanity couldn't care less if it happened again. Would let it happen. Knowing some of humanity would even applaud. Believing there is no other way for Jews to survive. I want to shout it at them from the rooftops, to cry it out loud: you have never asked for enough! Zionism, at least as it's lived today, accepts anti-Semitism, says it's permanent in the world: As long as there are Jews, there will be Jew-haters, Jew-killers, so we'll build a wall of bodies around us and live behind it, a menace to our neighbors, trying to feel safe. I stand here and cry out to you: "Come out of the trenches! Ask for it all! I demand for myself, and my children who will also be Jews, and for you, too, my soldiering kin, a world where fortresses are unknown and unnecessary."

11.

Of course we didn't give it up all by ourselves. There were the crisp upperclass British statesmen, steeped in generations of anti-Semitic lore, those smooth American diplomats who would never allow their daughters to marry one, those same men who knew what smoke that was that rose from the forests of Europe, who refused to bomb the camps in spite of plea after smuggled-out plea from the imprisoned Jews: "Bomb the camp! Kill us, please—as long as you destroy the ovens we will be glad. We can only die once. Let us take this hell on earth with us." These same men, suddenly righteous in the cause of the Jews, suddenly eager to settle them, to wrest land for them from the hands of others declaiming about the righting of outrageous wrongs, about humanitarian and disinterested love. Calculating the usefulness of a fortress in this place, cynically using the terror of the surviving Jews to build themselves the conditions of control.

12.

The mark of Abel, the sign of damage: that we cannot trust, expect nothing from our neighbors, turn away from the offered hand with a shudder, waiting for the blow to fall, for betrayal to come. We believe this is wisdom. We call it "having learned our lesson." We feel that it will kill us to ask for help outside the walls of this house. Yet we could be allies, the Arabs and we, two persecuted peoples rooted in the same land, the same customs, food, language. The task is the most difficult one, the most terrifying, the one requiring the most daring leap from the cliff of this present bloody moment.

For the Palestinians, the Lebanese, the other Arab peoples to see the impact of Jewish history on our lives, to see the Jews as people fleeing oppression, in need of allies, desperate for a piece of land from

which we cannot be driven. A place of our own to stand. Utterly believing we will die if we don't get it NOW. To hold this knowledge,
with compassion, even as they battle the Israeli soldier wherever he
sets his booted foot, refusing to pay the price for a pain they did
not create.

For Israeli Jews, for all Jews, to make the choice to step beyond fear,
to train our allies instead of fleeing them. To refuse to continue repeat-
ing, in the name of our terror, this cycle of tortures and massacres,
assassinations, exiles, and retaliations. To hold tightly to our right
to a piece of ground, to a nation among nations, and in that moment to finally understand that our safety does, in fact, depend on
theirs. Their nationhood an echo of our own. Even as we protect ourselves, to begin expecting, not the worst this time, but the best: that
the Arab peoples of the world will themselves say *never again*.

The most difficult task. In the midst of gunfire and slaughter and
anguish to imagine a peace built on kinship, on true alliance, side
by side, for each other and for ourselves. I know I have dreamt this
dream: Jews and Arabs moving in unison, dispossessing the warri-
ors, building new villages on the sites of the old, changing the face
of the land, the shape of history, the look of the future.

13.

I want to see a flowering of Arab and Jewish cultures in a country
without racism or anti-Semitism, without rich or poor or spat-upon:
everyone beneath the vine and fig tree living in peace and unafraid.
A homeland for each and every one of us between the mountains
and the sea. A multilingual, multireligious, many-colored and -peopled
land where the orange tree blooms for all. I will not surrender this
vision for any lesser compromise. No separate-but-equal armed camps
turning their backs on each other across a pitted buffer zone. No
Palestinian exile burning with dreams of return, injustice embitter-
ing generations of children who yearn always for the place of their
ancestors: next year in the Galilee. No graveyard the size of a nation,

Palestinian blood burning the ground and steaming up each morning, reeking of death. No fortress-state of Jews against all the rest of the world, generations of children growing up soldiers, believing themselves holy, believing there is no one outside the walls, believing fear is the only force that binds people together. I will accept nothing less than freedom.

It is not demanded of us that we complete the work of freedom (so it is written in the ancient texts of Hebrew wisdom), only that we begin it. This is where I begin. Here where the terror and the hope are, where the words pour out of me. There will be days and years ahead, I know this, of talk and work and battling out each step to take and how to take it and with whom; victories to win over the most rigid and terrified of our leaders and the damage we carry inside ourselves. But through it all, in the face of hatred and terror and factionalism, in the face of every urge to the safety of the halfway, I pledge to hold the vision clear and close. For if I forget thee, oh Jerusalem, my hands will have forgotten their uses, and my heart will be dumb, if I hold not our liberation above all other joy.

Ending

Ending Poem

I am what I am.
A child of the Americas.
A light-skinned mestiza of the Caribbean.
A child of many diaspora, born into this continent at a crossroads.
I am Puerto Rican. I am U.S. American.
I am New York Manhattan and the Bronx.
A mountain-born, country-bred, homegrown jíbara child,
up from the shtetl, a California Puerto Rican Jew.
A product of the New York ghettos I have never known.
I am an immigrant
and the daughter and granddaughter of immigrants.
We didn't know our forbears' names with a certainty.
They aren't written anywhere.
First names only, or mija, negra, ne, honey, sugar, dear.

I come from the dirt where the cane was grown.
My people didn't go to dinner parties. They weren't invited.
I am caribeña, island grown.
Spanish is in my flesh, ripples from my tongue, lodges in my hips,
the language of garlic and mangoes.
Boricua. As Boricuas come from the isle of Manhattan.
I am of latinoamerica, rooted in the history of my continent.
I speak from that body. Just brown and pink and full of drums inside.

I am not African.
Africa waters the roots of my tree, but I cannot return.

I am not Taína.
I am a late leaf of that ancient tree,
and my roots reach into the soil of two Americas.
Taíno is in me, but there is no way back.

I am not European, though I have dreamt of those cities.
Each plate is different,
wood, clay, papier mâché, metal, basketry, a leaf, a coconut shell.
Europe lives in me but I have no home there.

The table has a cloth woven by one, dyed by another,
embroidered by another still.
I am a child of many mothers.
They have kept it all going
All the civilizations erected on their backs.
All the dinner parties given with their labor.

We are new.
They gave us life, kept us going,
brought us to where we are.
Born at a crossroads.
Come, lay that dishcloth down. Eat, dear, eat.
History made us.
We will not eat ourselves up inside anymore.

And we are whole.

Other titles from Firebrand Books include:

Artemis In Echo Park, Poetry by Eloise Klein Healy/$8.95
Before Our Eyes, A Novel by Joan Alden/$8.95
Beneath My Heart, Poetry by Janice Gould/$8.95
The Big Mama Stories by Shay Youngblood/$8.95
The Black Back-Ups, Poetry by Kate Rushin/$9.95
A Burst Of Light, Essays by Audre Lorde/$9.95
Cecile, Stories by Ruthann Robson/$8.95
Crime Against Nature, Poetry by Minnie Bruce Pratt/$8.95
Diamonds Are A Dyke's Best Friend by Yvonne Zipter/$9.95
Dykes To Watch Out For, Cartoons by Alison Bechdel/$8.95
Dykes To Watch Out For: The Sequel, Cartoons by Alison Bechdel/$10.95
Eight Bullets by Claudia Brenner with Hannah Ashley/$12.95
Exile In The Promised Land, A Memoir by Marcia Freedman/$8.95
Experimental Love, Poetry by Cheryl Clarke/$8.95
Eye Of A Hurricane, Stories by Ruthann Robson/$8.95
The Fires Of Bride, A Novel by Ellen Galford/$8.95
Food & Spirits, Stories by Beth Brant (*Degonwadonti*)/$8.95
Forty-Three Septembers, Essays by Jewelle Gomez/$10.95
Free Ride, A Novel by Marilyn Gayle/$9.95
A Gathering Of Spirit, A Collection by North American Indian Women
    edited by Beth Brant (*Degonwadonti*)/$13.95
The Gilda Stories, A Novel by Jewelle Gomez/$10.95
Good Enough To Eat, A Novel by Lesléa Newman/$10.95
Horseshoe Sky, A Novel by Catherine Koger/$10.95
Humid Pitch, Narrative Poetry by Cheryl Clarke/$8.95
Jewish Women's Call For Peace edited by Rita Falbel, Irena Klepfisz, and
    Donna Nevel/$4.95
Jonestown & Other Madness, Poetry by Pat Parker/$7.95
Just Say Yes, A Novel by Judith McDaniel/$10.95
The Land Of Look Behind, Prose and Poetry by Michelle Cliff/$8.95
Legal Tender, A Mystery by Marion Foster/$9.95
Lesbian (Out)law, Survival Under the Rule of Law by Ruthann Robson/$9.95
A Letter To Harvey Milk, Short Stories by Lesléa Newman/$9.95
Letting In The Night, A Novel by Joan Lindau/$8.95
Living As A Lesbian, Poetry by Cheryl Clarke/$7.95
Metamorphosis, Reflections on Recovery by Judith McDaniel/$7.95
Mohawk Trail by Beth Brant (*Degonwadonti*)/$7.95
Moll Cutpurse, A Novel by Ellen Galford/$7.95
The Monarchs Are Flying, A Novel by Marion Foster/$8.95
More Dykes To Watch Out For, Cartoons by Alison Bechdel/$9.95
Movement In Black, Poetry by Pat Parker/$8.95
My Mama's Dead Squirrel, Lesbian Essays on Southern Culture by
    Mab Segrest/ $9.95
New, Improved! Dykes To Watch Out For, Cartoons by Alison Bechdel/$8.95
Normal Sex by Linda Smukler/$8.95
Now Poof She Is Gone, Poetry by Wendy Rose/$8.95

Oral Tradition, Selected Poems by Jewelle Gomez/$9.95

The Other Sappho, A Novel by Ellen Frye/$8.95

Out In The World, International Lesbian Organizing by Shelley Anderson/$4.95

Parker & Hulme: A Lesbian View by Julie Glamuzina and Alison J. Laurie /$12.95

Politics Of The Heart, A Lesbian Parenting Anthology edited by Sandra Pollack and Jeanne Vaughn/$12.95

Post-Diagnosis by Sandra Steingraber/$9.95

Presenting...Sister NoBlues by Hattie Gossett/$8.95

Rebellion, Essays 1980–1991 by Minnie Bruce Pratt/$12.95

Restoring The Color Of Roses by Barrie Jean Borich/$9.95

A Restricted Country by Joan Nestle/$9.95

Running Fiercely Toward A High Thin Sound, A Novel by Judith Katz/$9.95

Sacred Space by Geraldine Hatch Hanon/$9.95

Sanctuary, A Journey by Judith McDaniel/$7.95

Sans Souci, And Other Stories by Dionne Brand/$8.95

Scuttlebutt, A Novel by Jana Williams/$8.95

S/he by Minnie Bruce Pratt/$10.95

Shoulders, A Novel by Georgia Cotrell/$9.95

Simple Songs, Stories by Vickie Sears/$8.95

Sister Safety Pin, A Novel by Lorrie Sprecher/$9.95

Skin: Talking About Sex, Class & Literature by Dorothy Allison/$14.95

Spawn Of Dykes To Watch Out For, Cartoons by Alison Bechdel/$10.95

Speaking Dreams, Science Fiction by Severna Park/$9.95

Stardust Bound, A Novel by Karen Cadora/$8.95

Staying The Distance, A Novel by Franci McMahon/$9.95

Stone Butch Blues, A Novel by Leslie Feinberg/$12.95

The Sun Is Not Merciful, Short Stories by Anna Lee Walters/$8.95

Talking Indian, Reflections on Survival and Writing by Anna Lee Walters/$13.95

Tender Warriors, A Novel by Rachel Guido deVries/$8.95

This Is About Incest by Margaret Randall/$8.95

The Threshing Floor, Short Stories by Barbara Burford/$7.95

Trash, Stories by Dorothy Allison/$9.95

Unnatural Dykes To Watch Out For, Cartoons by Alison Bechdel/$10.95

We Say We Love Each Other, Poetry by Minnie Bruce Pratt/$8.95

The Women Who Hate Me, Poetry by Dorothy Allison/$8.95

Words To The Wise, A Writer's Guide to Feminist and Lesbian Periodicals & Publishers by Andrea Fleck Clardy/$5.95

The Worry Girl, Stories from a Childhood by Andrea Freud Loewenstein/$8.95

Yours In Struggle, Three Feminist Perspectives on Anti-Semitism and Racism by Elly Bulkin, Minnie Bruce Pratt, and Barbara Smith/$9.95

You can buy Firebrand titles at your bookstore, or order them directly from the publisher (141 The Commons, Ithaca, New York 14850, 607-272-0000).

Please include $3.00 shipping for the first book and $.50 for each additional book.

A free catalog is available on request.